THE COUNTRY HOUSE GARDEN
A Grand Tour

THE NATIONAL TRUST

THE COUNTRY HOUSE GARDEN

A GRAND TOUR

Text by
Gervase Jackson-Stops

Photographs by
James Pipkin

PAVILION

This edition first published in Great Britain in 1988 by
Pavilion Books Limited
196 Shaftesbury Avenue, London WC2H 8JL

First published in hardback in 1987

Text © Gervase Jackson-Stops 1987
Photographs © James Pipkin 1987

Designed by Bernard Higton

A CIP record for this book is available from
the British Library

ISBN 1 85145 123 4 (hbk)
ISBN 1 85145 441 1 (pbk)

Printed and bound in Italy by Arnoldo Mondadori

10   9   8   7   6   5   4   3   2

Frontispiece: The Water Garden at Blenheim Palace, created by Achille Duchêne
for the 9th Duke of Marlborough between 1925 and 1928.

CONTENTS

PREFACE

The *Treasure Houses of Britain* exhibition held at the National Gallery of Art in Washington in 1985-86 drew attention as never before to the immense cultural significance of the country house. While the catalogue was naturally devoted to its history as a focus of patronage and art-collecting over five centuries, our companion book, *The English Country House – A Grand Tour*, tried to give an idea of its architectural setting, room by room, examining the sequence of state apartments as they developed from the beginning of the Tudor to the end of the Hanoverian periods.

This book is intended to treat the wider garden and landscape setting of the country house in much the same way, examining in turn the different elements to be found on the circuit walk as opposed to the enfilade – marvels of topiary to match the elaborate flying testers of Baroque state beds, lakes and cascades to reflect the silver salvers and wine fountains of the dining-room *buffet*, flower gardens to rival the brilliant hues of crimson and green silk-damask walls.

The importance of the garden as an integral part of the country house has been a recurring theme in art throughout the ages, from the Montacute *millefleurs* tapestry suggesting the 'flowery meads' of the medieval garden, to Sir John Lavery's *Family Group at St Fagan's*, an Edwardian tea party on the terrace, with all the nostalgia of Henry James' *English Hours*. Formal layouts are depicted in Griffier's *View of Syon* and the famous *Presentation of a Pineapple to Charles II*, while Delft tulip vases and flower pieces by Monnoyer helped bring the Baroque garden indoors. Then there are the views of Chiswick by Rysbrack and Lambert showing William Kent's move towards an informal 'Picturesque' style of gardening in the early eighteenth century, followed by landscapes by the Old Masters – Claude, Poussin and Salvator Rosa, Cuyp and Ruysdael – which conditioned the taste of the later 'Natural Landscape' School. Thomas Robins' charming watercolour of Davenport, a design by 'Capability' Brown and one of Repton's 'Red Books' show the progress of this movement towards the *jardin anglais*, while Thomas Daniell's *View of West Wycombe* portrays a house so totally subservient to its setting that its façades were conceived as a series of garden buildings or 'eye-catchers' rather than as an architectural entity – looking forward to the full-blown romanticism of Turner's *Tabley House and Lake: Windy Day*. Even ceramics with the

Chelsea pastoral groups, Hans Sloane botanical plates, and views of famous gardens on Wedgwood and Worcester pieces, underline the country-house owner's passion for horticulture.

Although the gardens illustrated in this book have been carefully picked as archetypes of a particular style or date, it is obviously much rarer to find the 'untouched' here than inside the country house, where decorative schemes of the sixteenth or seventeenth centuries can still be found intact. Gardens are in a constant state of evolution, either decaying through neglect or changing through fashion, the availability of labour and machinery, or even natural conditions. Thus, even in a relatively modern garden like Sissinghurst, which the National Trust is pledged to keep as it was in V. Sackville-West's day, the carpet of polyanthus that was such a striking feature of the nuttery has now impoverished the soil to the point where it has had to be replaced by other plants, giving a very different effect – at least for the time being.

Reconstruction of the gardens of the past can never be wholly accurate. But whether looking at the Elizabethan garden through 1930s spectacles – as at Packwood – or the seventeenth-century Anglo-Dutch garden through 1970s spectacles – as at Westbury – the spirit of the original can be hauntingly evoked, and the old bird's-eye views, the parterres proudly depicted in the backgrounds of ancient family portraits, or the sylvan scenes of faded Mortlake tapestries, can come startlingly to life.

The renewed interest in garden history as an academic discipline has helped to establish greater accuracy in recent years, as can be seen in the restorations of formal layouts like Hatfield and Ham, as much as informal landscapes like Claremont and Painshill. At the same time it has helped to identify many rare features of early garden layouts that still survive even in the unlikely surroundings of a public park – from beds of flowers in the shape of giant baskets, derived from Repton, to the floral clock, so dear to the mayor and corporation, that goes back to the clipped box sundial of the sixteenth century.

This book owes much to the pioneering studies that have appeared in *Garden History* since 1972, and more recently in the *Journal of Garden History*, and to books like Roy Strong's *Renaissance Garden in England*, and Peter Willis and John Dixon Hunt's *Genius of the Place*, with its very useful anthology of writers on the subject between 1620 and 1820. Less space is devoted to planting, always the most ephemeral aspect of gardening, than to more permanent architectural elements like gates and gatepiers, lawns and terraces, statues and urns, canals and cascades. But so many books have appeared on the purely horticultural aspect of the country-house garden in recent years that no apology need be offered for this natural bias.

Once more it has been a pleasure to work with James Pipkin, whose photographs have caught the magic of the British summer despite its notorious unreliability, and whose eye for the unusual viewpoint and the telling detail have never in my experience been equalled. My thanks are also due to the National Trust's Gardens Adviser, John Sales, for much helpful advice, and to Maggie Grieve who brought this book, like its predecessor, to the light of day.

For the rest, I can only echo John Evelyn's letter to Sir Thomas Browne, written in 1657 to explain his projected (but never completed) *Elysium Britannicum*:

'The truth is, that which imported me to discourse on this subject after this sorte, was the many defects which I encounter'd in Bookes and in Gardens, wherein neither words nor cost had bin wanting, but judgement very much; and though I cannot boast of my science in this kind, as both unbecoming my yeares and my small experience, yet I esteem'd it pardonable at least, if in doing my endeavour to rectifie some mistakes, and advancing so usefull and innocent a divertisement, I made some essay, and cast in my Symbole with the rest. To this designe, if forraine observation may conduce, I might likewise hope to refine upon some particulars, especially concerning the ornaments of Gardens, which I shall endeavour so to handle, as that they may become usefull and practicable, as well as magnificent, and that persons of all conditions and faculties, which delight in Gardens, may therein encounter something for their owne advantage.'

Gervase Jackson-Stops

THE HOUSE IN ITS SETTING

'God Almightie first Planted a Garden', the famous opening words of Francis Bacon's essay 'Of Gardens', published in 1625, are a reminder of one of the oldest myths in the history of the world – the natural order represented by the Garden of Eden before the Fall, a place of lost innocence for which men have yearned for many thousands of years. It could be said that the search for the groves of Eden or the pastures of Arcadia, whether Christian or Classical in origin, lies at the very heart of the human psyche. The man-made garden thus has its origins not simply as a utilitarian means of providing food, but as an ideal setting for domestic life, a vision that may have taken very different forms over the centuries, but which has retained its promise, renewed with the buds of each succeeding spring.

The Scottish fortress and its garden: (above) the simple woodland setting of Craigievar, Aberdeenshire; (left) the formal splendour of Drummond Castle, Perthshire.

*C*hirk Castle, on the Welsh border, begun in 1295. The elaborate gardens
laid out round it in the seventeenth century were swept away by Capability Brown's
contemporary, William Emes, between 1761 and 1774.

For the Islamic world, the source of so many traditions in European horticulture, the garden was and is a place of enclosure, a walled oasis whose green shade offers a sanctuary from the merciless heat of the surrounding desert. The *hortus conclusus*, whether belonging to the castle or the monastery, followed the same principle, fortified both against hostile nature and against hostile human forces in an age of almost perpetual warfare. Like the stone arcades of the cloister, its tunnel-like arbours surrounding a central lawn planted with pears, cherries and medlars, provided a shady walk in fine weather – especially intended for the ladies of the household, at a time when the separation of the sexes also followed oriental practice. Diminutive gardens of this sort, often with a central wall or fountain, would usually be found within the castle walls, bordered by buildings on two or more sides, and with no relationship to the surrounding landscape.

Until the late sixteenth century, the choice of site for a house would depend almost entirely on how well it could be fortified, or how well it was supplied with water, and gardens appear to have been very much an afterthought. In the north of England and Scotland, where castles were usually built on high ground, the harsh climate encouraged the establishment of walled gardens on south-facing slopes some way away from the house, and this continued to be the normal practice even in the seventeenth and eighteenth centuries.

In the south, where the surroundings were likely to be less rugged, the old idea of the *hortus conclusus* was developed under the Tudors into a series of separate, enclosed gardens closely adjoining the house, whose emblematic tableaux could be 'read' from the windows of the state rooms high up at the top of the building. Slowly, the influence of the Italian Renaissance came to be felt, and with it the idea that, just as man lay at the centre of creation, so his house should be surrounded by gardens forming a miniature cosmos.

Alberti's *De re aedificatoria*, published in 1452 but little known in England till the following century, was of immense importance in gathering together for the first time all the classical references to gardens, including Pliny's famous descriptions of his villas at Tusculum and Laurentum. According to Alberti, the garden should be an extension of the house, expressed by geometrical design, and thus the province of the architect. Perhaps the first English garden to follow these precepts was at Wollaton in Nottinghamshire, built by Robert Smythson for Sir Francis Willoughby in the 1580s, with eight square enclosures laid out round the house, exactly corresponding with it in

Blair Castle in the Scottish Highlands, dominating the wide valley of Glen Tilt.

size. Few other Elizabethan houses were planned as an architectural unit with their gardens, but the relationship between the two was often stressed by the Italianate device of a loggia. At Wimbledon in Surrey and at Castle Ashby in Northamptonshire, these were placed on the side elevation overlooking the 'privy garden', but they could also be on the main garden front, as at Cranborne in Dorset.

The difference between the 'great garden' and the 'privy garden' precisely reflected the difference between the state rooms and the private apartments within the house: the first open to a vast concourse of household attendants, visitors and hangers-on; the second reserved only for the use of the family and the highest-ranking of their guests. At the 'prodigy houses' of great courtiers, like Sir Christopher Hatton's Holdenby, the gardens were also conceived like their counterpart rooms as a setting for masques and entertainments on a huge scale, their precise geometry reflecting the movements of the dances, and their symbolism reinforcing the tributes to Elizabeth I – whether as Astræa, the Virgin Queen, Diana the chaste huntress, or in one of her other allegorical personae.

Powis Castle in North Wales, overlooking William Winde's seventeenth-century terraces.

In the 1630s and '40s the axial geometry of the garden in relation to the house grew stronger. At Wilton, near Salisbury, the revolutionary Palladian architecture of the south front was matched by a garden like those of the Venetian villas on the Brenta, extending the whole width of the house, with a central axial path leading down to the river Avon. Another group of houses, including Little Hadham in Hertfordshire and Sir John Danvers' house in Chelsea, carried this a stage further with the parterre surrounded by raised terraces on all four sides, that opposite the house with an elaborate central staircase and corner pavilions balancing the architectural weight of the main building.

On the whole, the effect of these gardens was static, however, and it was only in the Baroque period that the newly fashionable enfilades, imparting a sense of movement inside the house, found an equivalent in the radiating *allées* and vistas outside. Advances in the understanding of optics were behind this development, just as they influenced the increasingly three-dimensional compositions of painters, like the *trompes l'oeil* of Samuel Hoogstraeten and the 'bird's-eye' views of parks and gardens by Jan

Siberechts. The *patte d'oie* or 'goose-foot' arrangement of avenues converging on the house, first introduced to England by the French gardener André Mollet, opened the way to a series of interconnecting spaces, all linked to the house – in the same way that hunting lodges like Ashdown in Berkshire had been placed at the centre of a star-shaped system of straight rides cut through the forest, affording spectators on the roof a view of the sport, and emphasizing the dominance of the house over the surrounding landscape.

Elizabethan hunting lodges, like Hardwick, were also among the first unfortified country houses to be built on hilltops. Less exposed situations were generally favoured throughout the seventeenth and early eighteenth centuries – Sir William Temple extolled the gently sloping site of Moor Park in Hertfordshire, and Timothy Nourse in his *Campania Foelix* (1700) recommended that a nobleman's seat should be erected 'not amongst Enclosures, but in a champaign, open Country'. Lord Tankerville's Uppark, built in the 1690s, high up on the Sussex Downs with distant views of the English Channel, is an exception to the rule, however, looking forward to the time when untamed nature would be admired rather than feared.

In Holland, where the small scale of estates rarely suited the limitless vistas of Le Nôtre, a much more static, compartmented garden, bounded by straight canals was the order of the day: the house itself occupying a central position only in the French-influenced palaces of William III and his immediate circle. Although Dutch influence can be strongly felt in the Gloucestershire gardens of Westbury and Dyrham, the Baroque parterres of William and Mary's English supporters likewise looked to France rather than the Low Countries for inspiration.

William Winde's great terraces at Cliveden in Buckinghamshire and Powis in North Wales are echoes of Saint-Germain, with martial overtones suitable for Lord Orkney, Britain's first Field-Marshal, and for the Herberts, who had inherited the greatest of the Welsh border fortresses. Vauban's forts were also the decisive influence on the gardens created by Sir John Vanbrugh in partnership with Charles Bridgeman at Blenheim, Grimsthorpe and Eastbury: their ramparts and bastions not only in keeping with the 'castle air' of Vanbrugh's houses, but also offering views into the neighbouring countryside, previously blocked by high boundary walls.

'The capital stroke, the leading step to all that has followed,' in Horace Walpole's words, was the introduction of another feature with a military origin: the sunk fence or 'ha-ha'. 'No sooner was this simple enchantment made,' he wrote in his *History of the Modern Taste in Gardening*, 'than levelling, mowing and rolling followed. The . . . park without the sunk fence was to be harmonised with the lawn within, and the garden in its turn was to be set free from its prim regularity, that it might assort with the wilder country without.' For Walpole, the undoubted hero of the hour was William Kent, who 'leaped the fence, and saw that all nature was a garden.' In fact Kent was by no means the first to use the ha-ha – Monsieur Beaumont, Colonel Graham's French gardener at Levens, had already made one there in the 1690s – and although Kent was undoubtedly the leading exponent of the early 'natural landscape' garden, there were many other economic, political and intellectual reasons for the revolution in taste which took Britain on such a different path to her Continental neighbours in the eighteenth century.

Under the Tudors, the dissolution of the monasteries and the enclosure system had already led to the creation of large landed estates, mostly supported by cattle- and sheep-grazing in place of the intensive arable farming that continued elsewhere in Europe. A new breed of resident landowners, who, unlike their counterparts in France and Germany, only rarely visited the capital and the court, also saw the commercial possibilities of woodlands, taking the advice of John Evelyn's *Sylva* (1664) and planting their demesnes with 'trees of venerable shade and profitable timber'. The many new species imported from the Mediterranean countries, from Scandinavia and America, also added to the colour and interest of the countryside beyond the garden walls.

A new style of gardening which was wholly compatible with existing agricultural practice, in Pope's words 'calling in the country', was bound to appeal to a class which identified so strongly with its lands. The economies to be made, compared with the upkeep of the formal garden, have perhaps been overstressed: Thomas Jefferson found fifteen men and eighteen boys at work at Stowe, and two hundred at Blenheim – fifty of them working on the Pleasure Grounds alone – while armies of men were needed for the levelling of hills and digging of lakes ordered by Capability Brown. But against this could be set the huge increases in the size of gardens, reflecting the ever-greater power of the Whig oligarchy.

The political and literary background of the 'Picturesque' movement was just as important as the economic. Rejecting the Baroque style of architecture as an expression of foreign absolutism, Lord Burlington and his followers proposed a return to the villas of classical antiquity, as described by Vitruvius, and interpreted by Palladio and

Inigo Jones. In very much the same way, they looked on the regimented lines of the Baroque garden (above all the perfect symmetry of Versailles) as a restriction of natural liberties, and urged a return to the landscapes described by the classical authors, notably Virgil, and interpreted by the painters Claude and Poussin. Balance was the quality they particularly sought – whether between hills and water, trees and bridges, temples and ruins, or even between square buildings and round ones – and this too had political connotations, for it was often held to express the balanced powers of the British constitution. The lack of variety in a formal layout, where the entire garden could be seen in one view from the main terrace, was also something to be avoided.

Instead of being the epicentre of the garden, the Palladian house gradually became no more than an incident within it. The idea of the circuit walk 'made through a succession of pictures', as Walpole put it, obviously started and ended with the house, and views back to it from different angles were composed with the greatest care to achieve a painterly effect. But smaller garden buildings, surprise views down on to lakes or rivers, cascades like Ruysdael's or hovels like Salvator Rosa's, could form equally satisfactory subjects. At Stourhead and at Studley Royal, two of the most famous 'Picturesque' landscapes, the house was actually situated outside the garden and could be seen from nowhere on the circuit walk. Elsewhere, its façades were treated as individual 'eyecatchers' to be spotted at different stages in the tour of the garden, like Nicholas Revett's portico at West Wycombe, always known as the 'Temple of Bacchus'. Richard Payne Knight even went so far as to remodel Downton Castle in Wiltshire so that it should look like the irregular, partly castellated farmhouses familiar from the landscapes of Claude, set high on its bluff above the river Wye, while in the 1830s the Husseys reduced their old castle at Scotney to a shell, and commissioned Salvin to build a new house on the hill above, with a terrace by William Sawrey Gilpin specially contrived to frame the newly picturesque ruin.

The total subservience of the house to its surroundings was stressed in two contrasting engravings in Payne Knight's *The Landscape*, published in 1794: the first showing a typical Georgian sash-windowed block set in a rather bleak parkland setting, with clumps of trees (which cattle have shorn of their lower branches) and a serpentine lake in the manner of Capability Brown; the second a much wilder scene of shaggy trees and boulders, with a rushing torrent, and the house beyond, remodelled as a 'Tudorbethan' pile, its skyline bristling with towers, obelisks and chimneystacks. Early in his career, Humphry Repton subscribed wholeheartedly to such principles –

*Three centuries of growth: William Nesfield's parterre at
Blickling, laid out in 1872 and simplified by Norah Lindsay in the 1930s – with the early
eighteenth-century woodland garden and Doric Temple beyond.*

*T*he 'green parterre' on a huge scale, complementing the architecture of the country house: (above) a view from the roof of Cliveden in
Buckinghamshire, with the river Thames in the background; (below) a view from the parapet at Chatsworth in Derbyshire,
with the river Derwent beyond. To Garibaldi, who stayed at Cliveden in 1864, the very different vista of the Thames from Canning's
oak (right) recalled 'some of the mightiest river prospects of South America'.

*T*he old castle at Scotney in Kent, seen from the terrace of Salvin's new house,
built in the 1830s: a quintessential statement of 'picturesque' principles, achieved with
the help of the landscape gardener, William Sawrey Gilpin.

for instance advising that towers of different heights be added to Blaise Castle in 1796. But by 1805 he was recommending a symmetrical arrangement of balustrade and flower-filled urns between the projecting wings of the garden front at Wimpole: in other words, bringing back formality to the immediate environs of the house.

The so-called 'gardenesque' style advocated by J. C. Loudon in the 1820s took this a stage further. Loudon had also begun as a thoroughgoing 'Picturesque' gardener following the principles of Payne Knight and Uvedale Price, but his extensive tours of the Continent between 1811 and 1821 and his conversion to the theories of Quatre-mère de Quincy, convinced him that gardens should be consciously differentiated from wild nature and recognizable as works of art. In his *Encyclopedia of Gardening* (1822) he also laid down the principle that each plant should be displayed to its best advantage. The vast numbers of new species and hybrids now being imported from every quarter of the globe, and cultivated in increasingly efficient hothouses, thus led to the eclecticism of Victorian garden design – the revival of formal parterres near the house, filled with bedding plants of brilliant hues and overlooked by Italianate terraces and steps; the rockeries for Alpine plants; the Japanese water gardens; the American shrubberies; the ferneries and pinetums – that still give gardens like Biddulph Grange and Alton Towers the feeling of horticultural museums, divided into type.

The 'Picturesque' style never entirely died – indeed in some respects it reached its apogee with houses like Cragside in Northumberland, perched above a ravine in a landscape, soon transformed from a lunar waste into a romantic fir-forest worthy of the brothers Grimm. But more often it was watered down to suit the tastes of plants-men like William Robinson and his 'Surrey School', proud of the fact that their gardens grew out of the site and were never committed to plans on paper. This attitude was fiercely opposed by the architect Reginald Blomfield, following in the steps of Sir Charles Barry's great formal terraces at Trentham, Harewood and Shrubland, and in turn influencing Harold Peto's Buscot and Sir George Sitwell's Renishaw.

A synthesis between these opposite extremes was achieved by the partnership of an architect and a plantswoman, both of remarkable abilities: Edwin Lutyens and Gertrude Jekyll, who worked together on some seventy gardens between 1893 and 1912. Initially influenced by the Arts and Crafts movement and the cult of the cottage garden (which can be traced right back to the Regency period), Lutyens and Jekyll reintroduced a strong sense of unity between the vernacular house and its garden, successfully interlocking elements of their plan – a wing here, a pond there – by means of pergolas, loggias, steps and 'architectural' planting. 'Every garden scheme', Lutyens wrote, 'should have a backbone, a central idea beautifully phrased. Every wall, path, stone and flower should have its relationship to the central idea.' Lindisfarne off the Northumberland coast, Folly Farm in Berkshire and Hestercombe in Somerset are outstanding examples of their attention to detail, and use of local materials and traditions.

The two most famous gardens of the inter-war years, Laurence Johnston's Hidcote and V. Sackville-West's Sissinghurst, owe much to Gertrude Jekyll's restrained colour schemes, but also seem to evoke Dutch seventeenth-century designs in their strictly compartmented areas like 'outdoor rooms', each with a different character. Formal lines – tall yew hedges, pleached limes, walls, *clairvoyées* and rows of fruit trees – provide a foil for informal planting – herbaceous borders, ground cover, ornamental vegetables, clematis and rambling roses – to provide a mixture of grandeur and domesticity, rationalism and sentiment, in tune with the twentieth century's nostalgic view of the country house.

A setting for a Jacobean masque: the loggia at Cranborne Manor, Dorset.
(Right) A backdrop for a Victorian melodrama: the conifer woods at Cragside, Northumberland.

of immense antiquity. According to the Book of Genesis, 'a river went out of Eden to water the garden and from thence it was parted, and became four heads.' The *chahar bagh* or 'fourfold garden' of Islamic culture goes back to at least 6000 bc, evidently deriving from the same basic tradition, and it was from Persia, through the Byzantines, that the form was first introduced to Europe – together with the idea of raised banks or seats of turf, and surrounding borders of flowers. These enclosed gardens, often with four paths leading to a fountain at the centre, usually lay immediately below the windows of first-floor solars or chambers, and hence the need for a pleasing geometrical shape seen from above, which was to become one of the chief characteristics of the parterre. Interestingly, the cloister seems not to have contributed to its development (early monastic accounts speaking only of turf and the occasional tree), although the idea of tunnel-like arbours round the four sides of the parterre – derived above all from Burgundy – may be a reminiscence of its covered walks.

Early on, the different sections of the parterre were likely to be treated either as plain lawn or with different flowers sown broadcast in clover – the so-called 'flowery meads' familiar from French *millefleur* tapestries of the fifteenth century. The idea of patterns of 'knots' of interlacing bands (based on the symbol for infinity: ∞) caught on early in the sixteenth century, however, many of them influenced by Francesco Colonna's *Hypnerotomachia Poliphili*, published in Venice in 1499, with diagrams which the author related to *tapeti* or carpets. In a rare description of Henry VIII's privy garden at Hampton Court, the German Thomas Platter, exactly a hundred years later, noticed 'numerous patches where square cavities had been scooped out, as for paving stones; some of these were filled with red brick-dust, some with white sand, and some with green lawn, very much resembling a chess-board.' Similar knots at Richmond Palace in 1501 were made in the form of 'marvellous beasts, as lions, dragons, and such other of divers kinds, properly fashioned and carved in the ground, right well sanded, and compassed with lead.'

Gervase Markham, in *The English Husbandman* of 1613, differentiates between these 'open knots', where the pattern was set out in lines of rosemary, thyme or some other herb and the intervening spaces filled with coloured earth or sand, and 'closed knots' where the spaces were filled with flowers. The former seem already to have been going out of fashion by 1625, however, when Francis Bacon remarked that 'as for the making of knots or figures, with divers coloured earths that they may lie under the windows of the house on that side which the garden stands, they be but toys; you may see as good sights many times in tarts.' The effect of flowered knots, edged with box, can be better judged today from reconstructions like the west parterre at Hatfield House, where the planting is based on the surviving accounts of John Tradescant the first, Robert Cecil's famous gardener. Some walled Scottish gardens like Edzell and Pitmedden, because they lay so far away from the house, also escaped the 'improving hand' of the eighteenth century, and their restoration shows how the idea of the closed knot lingered on into the 1680s and 1690s, far away from the fashions of London.

Compared with earlier knot gardens, the main parterre at Somerset House, which Salomon de Caus began to lay out for Anne of Denmark in 1609, was revolutionary in that it treated all four sections or 'plotts' of the parterre as part of the same unified design, with a central path leading down to the Thames – a first advance towards axial Baroque planning. A bolder and larger-scale approach was also advocated by John Evelyn, who abhorred 'those painted and formal projections of our Cockney Gardens and plotts, which appear like Gardens of past board and March pane, and smell more of paint than of flowers and verdure,' but who admired the parterre at the Luxembourg in Paris, '. . . indeede of box; but so rarely designd, and accurately kept cut; that the embroidery makes a stupendious effect, to the lodgings which front it.'

The *parterre de broderie* which Evelyn saw had already influenced the garden at Wilton, laid out by the fourth Earl of Pembroke, an ex-ambassador to France, in the 1630s. But after the Restoration the form was to spread like wildfire, reaching a climax in the work of the Royal gardeners, London and Wise, at the end of the century. Its flowing plant-like designs were carried out in the simple materials of box, grass and bare earth – often enlivened with topiary and statues – and, although said to be based on needlework, also recall the acanthus patterns so popular with plasterers and wood-carvers within the 'double-pile' house. The east parterre at Blenheim, meticulously re-created by Achille Duchêne for the ninth Duke of Marlborough in the early years of this century, gives a good idea of a London and Wise *parterre de broderie*, otherwise known only from the bird's-eye views of Kip and Knyff's *Britannia Illustrata*.

In his translation of Dezallier d'Argenville's *Theory and Practice of Gardening* (1712), John James makes a distinction between parterres of embroidery and those of *compartiment*, where 'the same Symmetry of Design is repeated, as well in respect of the Ends, as of the Sides.' Bolder in their patterns, 'with Grassworks, Knots, and Borders of Flowers', these were generally placed beyond the more intricate *broderie* sections, and

The Great Garden at Pitmedden, Aberdeenshire, laid out in the second half of the seventeenth century by Sir Alexander Seton, and reconstructed since 1952.

James says that their paths were usually of 'Tile-shards powdered or Brick-dust', whereas the latter had no paths, and depended for contrast on the box foliage against sand and 'Smiths-Dust, or black Earth'. Two other plainer types he characterizes as the 'Cut-work' parterre, containing flower-beds bordered with box – not unlike the old 'closed knots', but described by him as 'not so fashionable at present' – and the *parterre à l'Angloise*, so-called because it was said to originate in England, and consisting of geometrical patterns cut in turf, with only a single border of flowers round it. These last were obviously much easier to maintain than the others, and became increasingly popular, but the grandest gardens, like Wanstead or Canons, had examples of all four, arranged in descending order of elaboration (and ascending order of scale) so as to achieve an effect of balance when seen all at once from the front of the house. Nor of course was any country-house garden complete without its bowling green – a feature also exported to France where it became the *boulingrin* – sometimes found in the main vista, but more often placed to one side of the parterre.

An early seventeenth-century pleasance at Edzell Castle, Angus, showing the walls with their original flower or nesting boxes.

Doubts had been expressed about the artificiality of the parterre as early as John Milton's *Paradise Lost* (1667), where the poet speaks of

> Flours worthy of paradise which not nice Art
> In Beds and curious Knots, but Nature boon
> Powrd forth profuse on Hill and Dale and Plaine.

Sir William Temple, in his *Gardens of Epicurus*, published in 1692, first drew attention to the wholly irregular beauty of Chinese gardens, coining the wonderful word 'Shara-wadgi' to describe them, but even he could not recommend his compatriots to try to emulate them – concluding that 'they are Adventures of too hard Achievement for any common Hands . . . whereas, in regular Figures [i.e. parterres], 'tis hard to make any great and remarkable Faults.' But the move toward simpler green parterres ('my quaker parter', as Lord Orkney described his huge garden set above the Thames at Cliveden in the 1720s) was soon to herald an abandonment of the whole principle of formal gardens, contrasted with the wildness of surrounding nature. Pope's celebrated verses in the *Epistle to Lord Burlington* administered the *coup de grâce*:

> His *Gardens* next your Admiration call,
> On ev'ry side you look behold the Wall!
> No pleasing Intricacies intervene,
> No artful wilderness to perplex the Scene:
> Grove nods at Grove, each Ally has a Brother,
> And half the Platform just reflects the other.

Looking at the vast numbers of elaborate parterres in the engravings of Kip and Knyff, Badeslade and Rocque, all of them to be swept away in the passion for 'natural landscape', it is hard to escape the conclusion that Capability Brown and his followers were destroyers on a grand scale. But there were few at the time who voiced any doubts. Perhaps the first inkling of a change of heart can be found in Horace Walpole's *History of the Modern Taste in Gardening* (1771), where he comments that 'the total banishment of all particular neatness immediately about a house, which is frequently left gazing by itself in the middle of a park, is a defect.'

Humphry Repton too felt that the standardization of the 'Picturesque' garden had gone too far. In his 'Red Book' for Wimpole, as early as 1801, he attacked 'the absurd fashion of bringing cattle to the windows of the house', and very soon he was urging a return to formal flower-beds and terraces in the immediate vicinity of a symmetrical, classical façade. One of the famous 'before-and-after' views in his *Fragments on the Theory and Practice of Landscape Gardening* (1816) shows White Lodge in Richmond Park, first in a scrubby heathland setting, with broken-down fences, and one of the ladies of the house being pursued by a bull – and then transformed, by the raising of a flap, into a scene of Regency elegance, with members of the family perambulating a broad central walk flanked by flower-beds and tall trellis-work arches. Francis Bacon's description of just such a 'Stately Arched Hedge . . . the Arches to be upon Pillars, of Carpenters Works, of some Ten Foot high, and Six Foot broad', shows that after two hundred years the wheel had turned full circle.

In their design, if not in their planting, many early nineteenth-century parterres were actually based on historical evidence. That at Drummond Castle in Perthshire, perhaps the finest formal garden of its type in Britain, was ostensibly a re-creation of the original seventeenth-century layout, based on the cross of St Andrew, Scotland's patron saint. But Lewis Kennedy, who worked on it from 1818 to 1860, introduced variegated evergreens, rose hedges and flowering shrubs to achieve a wholly different effect – very much a romantic's view of the old Scottish garden. In the same way, W. A. Nesfield, a successful painter before he took to garden design, often based his formal parterres on old pattern-books, like d'Argenville's *La Theorie et la practique du jardinage* (1709), but made them far bolder and more architectural in effect with Irish yews, terracotta balustrades and fountain basins.

The huge greenhouses of the time, and the armies of gardeners available, vastly increased the scale of 'bedding-out' – the system whereby parterre beds would be filled with different flowering plants for different times of the year. The pioneers of bedding in the 1830s were George Fleming at Trentham Park in Staffordshire and Donald Beaton at Shrubland Park in Suffolk, while the addition of spring bulbs to the repertoire was first introduced by John Fleming at Cliveden. Significantly, all three were great Italianate houses designed by Sir Charles Barry, and Barry's skill in providing the architectural framework for their horticultural experiments was of crucial importance for the development of the Victorian garden.

In the twentieth century, many of the great formal parterres were simplifed not only for economic reasons, but because the strident colours of pelargoniums, petunias, salvias and lobelias were going out of fashion. In their place, followers of Gertrude Jekyll like Norah Lindsay (who modified Nesfield's parterre at Blickling) substituted the perennials of the herbaceous border, carefully graded in size to achieve pyramid effects in each bed. At the same time carpet-bedding, using dwarf or creeping foliage plants in contrasting patterns, became increasingly the preserve of the municipal park, and was replaced by less complicated blocks of softer colour, using plants like santolina and senecio – as at Cliveden. New parterres are still being laid out, ranging from the west garden at Chatsworth, with the ground-plan of Lord Burlington's villa at Chiswick simply executed in cut box, to that at Holker in Cumbria, where ornamental cabbages and standard honeysuckles vie with more conventional annuals and perennials in the border. Here among busts and urns, garden seats and trellis obelisks – all symmetrically arranged round the smoothest of croquet lawns – they represent an eclectic, 1980s response to the old challenge of the formal parterre.

*S*ir William Bruce's gardens at Kinross in Fifeshire were planted and had become famous even before the great Scottish architect embarked on the rebuilding of the house. Sir Charles Lyttleton, writing from London in 1688, had heard that 'Lady Lauderdale's gardens at Ham are but a wilderness compared to yours'. Some of the main French-inspired features still survive, including the axial path aligned on an old island castle in Loch Leven.

*A romantic's view of the old Scottish garden:
the great parterre at Drummond Castle, Perthshire, recreated in the 1820s
and 1830s by George and Lewis Kennedy.
(Above) The view from the upper terrace, showing the overall plan in
the form of St Andrew's Cross. (Below) The fountain garden to the south-east.
(Left) The 'Crown', with flowering shrubs and variegated evergreens,
within box-edged beds.*

*P*eacocks on a balustrade at Dyrham Park in Gloucestershire. Perched on walls, or spreading their tails on great flights of steps, they have always been perfect foils to the formality of the parterre. (Right) Lady Salisbury's new knot garden at Cranborne Manor, Dorset, seen from an upstairs window – a modern design perfectly in harmony with the seventeenth-century house.

IV

TOPIARY AND MAZES

The art of topiary, shaping trees and shrubs by clipping them, expresses man's need to tame the wildness of nature at its most basic. The word derives ultimately from the Greek *topia* meaning landscapes, through the Latin *opus topiarium*, used to describe the whole art of ornamental gardening rather than in the narrower modern sense. However, Pliny the Elder refers in his *Naturalis Historia* to cypress trees being cut into tableaux – 'hunt-scenes, fleets of ships, and all sorts of images' – and ascribes the invention of tree-clipping to a Roman named G. Matius, active at the end of the first century bc. The younger Pliny's account of the garden at his Tuscan villa also mentions 'box, which is cut into a thousand shapes or even letters, which sometimes spell out the name of the owner, sometimes that of the designer.'

Topiary at Levens Hall, Cumbria (above and right) originally planted by the French gardener Guillaume Beaumont between 1689 and 1712.

In the Middle Ages, plants were sometimes trained on withy frames, for instance to shade the tunnel arbours round the edge of the *hortus conclusus*. But the first real revival of topiary came with the Italian Renaissance, and there is evidence to show that it was directly inspired by the study of the classical authors. Francesco Colonna's *Hypnerotomachia Poliphili* (1499), which was translated into English by Robert Dallington in 1592, illustrates not only simple topiary shapes like spheres and mushrooms, but also elaborate human figures, peacocks, towers and other architectural forms. According to Thomas Platter, writing in 1599, the privy garden at Hampton Court contained 'all manner of shapes, men and women, half men and half horse, sirens, serving-maids with baskets, French lilies and delicate crenellations all round made from dry twigs bound together and . . . evergreen quick-set shrubs, or entirely of rosemary, all true to the life, and so cleverly and amusingly interwoven, mingled and grown together, trimmed and arranged picture-wise that their equal would be difficult to find.' Extraordinary as it may seem, these amazing feats of topiary, inspired by fifteenth-century Italian gardens like that of the Rucellai in Florence, may well have dated back to Henry VIII's time, for his account-books of the 1530s are full of purchases of quicksets and of willow-branches or osiers with which to build them.

In the seventeenth century holly, yew, box, bay, laurel and phillyrea were all widely used for topiary subjects, although more abstract geometrical shapes now became popular, like the ovals, triangles, circles and orbs described as 'divine and moral remembrances' in the third Earl of Pembroke's garden at Wilton in the 1620s. Francis Bacon, in his essay 'Of Gardens' (1625), writes 'I for my part, do not like images cut out in juniper or other garden stuff – they be for children. Little low hedges round like welts, with some pretty pyramids I like well, and in some places fair columns.' No authentic topiary of this date has survived, but despite the fact that it is a nineteenth-century creation, the famous Yew Garden at Packwood House in Warwickshire, representing the Sermon on the Mount, captures the feeling of an early Stuart layout, in what Roy Strong has called its 'abstract moral geometry'. Among its towering pillars of yew – the four evangelists, the twelve apostles, and the 'multitude' below – one can understand the cleric who wrote to Ralph Austen, author of a book entitled *The Spiritual Use of a Garden*, published in 1652: 'I seldome come to your garden but what you made your trees *speak* something of Christ and the Gospel.'

The idea of the maze, too, was symbolic, representing man's quest for truth and enlightenment, and naturally looking back to one of the most potent myths of classical antiquity, the legend of the Cretan Minotaur. In Tudor England, they were carried out in low borders not unlike knot gardens, but labyrinths with taller hedges existed at Nonsuch and Theobalds by the end of the sixteenth century, the former so high that it was impossible to see from one path to another. Once again the immediate inspiration must have come from Italy and France. Du Pérac's well known engraving of the Villa d'Este, made in 1573, shows no less than four mazes, while the Cardinal d'Amboise had square and circular ones at the centre of his garden at Gaillon. In England, the maze was more likely to be on the outer extremities of the garden, though if possible on low ground where the overall plan could be seen from the windows of the house, as at Hatfield.

Sometimes they would be paired with 'wildernesses', and formed of beech or hornbeam rather than yew. The maze at Wimbledon House, laid out by André Mollet for Queen Henrietta Maria, was described by the Parliamentarian surveyors in 1649 as being made of 'young trees wood and sprayes of a good growth and height cutt out into severall meanders circles semicircles wynding and Intricate turnings the walkes or intervalls whereof are all grass plots'. Elsewhere, they were useful as shelter-belts: the triangular maze at Hampton Court, planted by Henry Wise for Queen Anne, was placed, in Defoe's words, 'on the North Side of the House, where the Gardens seem'd to want skreening from the Weather . . . and some Part of the old Building requir'd to be cover'd from the Eye.'

By the end of the seventeenth century, topiary was on the whole used as an ingredient in the different types of parterre, rather than to form a separate section of the garden. Stephen Switzer describes Dyrham Park in 1718 as having a 'Principal Gravel Walk, leading to the Main Door at the Front, being set off with large Pyramid Silver Hollies, Ews, &c. having painted Iron Rods with gilded Nobs for their Support', and the cross-walks lined with 'round-headed laurels exactly clipt, Bays, small pyramid Ews, &c.' Even the famous garden at Levens Hall in Cumbria, laid out for the Jacobite Colonel Graham by his French gardener Guillaume Beaumont between 1689 and 1712, must have begun life as a more conventional parterre (seen in early plans) before the yews were allowed to grow to a gigantic size at the end of the eighteenth century.

Celia Fiennes, visiting Woburn in the 1690s, reminds us that topiary was not confined to the garden, for in the 'fine parke full of deer and wood . . . some off the trees are kept cut in works and the shape of severall beasts'. Addison was to pour scorn on such artificiality in his *Spectator* articles. 'Our *British* Gardeners,' he wrote in 1712, 'instead of humouring Nature, love to deviate from it as much as possible. Our Trees rise in Cones, Globes and Pyramids. We see the Marks of the Scissars upon every Plant and Bush . . . but, for my own part, I would rather look upon a Tree in all its Luxuriancy and Diffusion of Boughs and Branches, than when it is cut and trimmed into a Mathematical Figure.' Pope's satirical 'Catalogue of Greens to be disposed of by an eminent Town-Gardiner' appeared the following year in the *Guardian*, and included such choice items as '*Adam* and *Eve* in Yew; *Adam* a little shatter'd by the fall of the Tree of Knowledge in the great Storm; *Eve* and the Serpent very flourishing'; 'The Tower of *Babel*, not yet finished'; 'A *Laurustine* Bear in Blossom, with a Juniper Hunter in Berries'; 'A Queen *Elizabeth* in Phylyraea, a little inclining to the Green Sickness, but of full growth'; 'A Quick-set Hog shot up into a Porcupine, by its being forgot a Week in rainy Weather'; and, lastly, 'A Pair of Maidenheads in Firr, in great forwardness'.

The use of topiary not so much for living sculpture as for 'hortulan architecture', in John Evelyn's phrase, was less controversial and longer-lasting, to judge by Pieter Rysbrack's paintings of the garden at Chiswick, and early views of Kent's Esher Place and Bridgeman's Claremont. However, even these tall hedges cut into 'colonnades', niches for statues, or 'green cabinets', were to be swept away in the 1740s as part of the overwhelming craze for the 'Picturesque'. By the time the fashion for topiary came to be resurrected in the early nineteenth century those few trees that still survived from the old Baroque layouts had been allowed to grow to enormous size and so lose much of their precise geometry – like the towering hedges surrounding the forecourt at Cirencester Park, or the huge domes of yew on the terraces at Powis Castle. Different as these were from the neat pyramids and spheres seen in the engravings of Kip and Knyff, they had a romantic appeal in their own right, summoning up the world of Walter Scott's *Kenilworth*, and the half-medieval, half-Elizabethan chivalry of the Eglinton Tournament.

In W. A. Nesfield's mid-Victorian parterres, topiary once again took its place as a major architectural element. Pillars of Irish yew (first discovered at Florence Court in Northern Ireland) continued the theme of porticoes and loggias in the house itself, and immaculately kept hedges, cut from great scaffolds using plumb lines, provided a perfect background for statuary, ponds or herbaceous borders. The Egyptian garden at Biddulph Grange in Staffordshire, dating from the 1850s, shows how successfully yew hedges could be made to create a whole stage-set, worthy of *Aida*, with only two pairs of stone sphinxes and a temple door to give it authenticity.

The old idea of clipping evergreens to the shape of birds and beasts may have been banished from the country house in the eighteenth century, but it clung on as a tradition in cottage gardens well into the nineteenth. Like the half-timbering and 'loveably dripping thatch' of the cottages themselves, it once more came into vogue with the Arts and Crafts movement, and topiary specimens are recommended in books like J. D. Sedding's *Garden Craft Old and New* (1891) and Reginald Blomfield's *The Formal Garden in England* (1892). The form of the peacocks at Great Dixter in Sussex, a fifteenth-century manor house repaired and enlarged by Lutyens in 1910, are taken straight from the homely 'front gardens' depicted in the watercolours of Helen Allingham and Kate Greenaway. But subtly abstracted, and repeated to form a group, they achieve a monumentality very different from the original.

Gertrude Jekyll's admiration for 'the splendid old yew hedge at Holme Lacy, like a weather-worn rock of vegetation, the surface clipped and yet showing something of its natural anatomy', can be paralleled by Lutyens' choice of antique furniture for his houses. For she felt that topiary should have the character of Tennyson's 'immemorial elms', supplying the patina of age in a garden, as well as perpetuating one of the most ancient of the gardener's skills. At Canons Ashby in Northamptonshire, Sir Henry Dryden used to line his male guests up on the terrace in the 1890s, to have their hair cut by the 'versatile person who was at once postman, barber, and the topiary artist who clipped the yews' – a combination of talents that would surely have delighted William Morris.

After the First World War, topiary may have become simpler in form, but yew and box hedges more than ever provided the architectural framework for the country house garden. At Hidcote and at Sissinghurst the yew hedges not only divided the layout into separate compartments, but provided an ideal background for the controlled colour schemes of herbaceous beds and borders, while box was used for edging and for smaller pyramids and hemispheres at the corners, where formality was called for. More recently standard honeysuckles and rosemaries clipped into balls, pyramid bays and Portugal laurels planted in Versailles tubs, and yew hedges with 'windows' cut through to give a view outside the confines of the garden, have signalled a return to still greater formality – based on an increasing interest in garden history. With symbolism and allegory back in fashion, who knows what curious shapes may yet emerge in the topiary of the twenty-first century?

The topiary garden at Packwood in Warwickshire (above and right) supposed to represent the Sermon on the Mount.
(Below) A set for Aida in clipped yew: the Egyptian garden at Biddulph Grange, Staffordshire, now being restored by the National Trust.

*S*olid walls of yew, overhung with cherry blossom, on the terraces at Powis Castle, North Wales.

*T*opiary as architecture: (above) the yew arbour at Drummond Castle, (below) the buttresses below the terrace at Pitmedden.

*T*he maze at Hever Castle (left), in the angle of the medieval moat, with the monogram of its
creator, William Waldorf Astor, planted in box at the entrance. (Above) A yew hedge with 'windows' at Cranborne
Manor, of a type known in France in the early eighteenth century as a 'Palissade de Chantilly'.
John James, who illustrated similar hedges in his <u>Theory and Practice of Gardening</u> (1712), urged their
use for 'Galleries, Porticoes, Halls and Green Vistas'.

*C*ottage-garden topiary in the White Garden at Hidcote (above) – praised by V. Sackville-West as being 'in the country tradition of smug broody hens, bumpy doves and coy peacocks' – contrasted with the simpler geometry of the 'brackets' round a square pool at Crathes Castle, Kincardineshire (left) planted in 1932, and (right) the stepped planes of yew surrounding the lily pond at Knightshayes in Devon.

V

FLOWER GARDENS AND BORDERS

Flowers have exercised a fascination for man from the beginning of time, despite the fact that they are of less practical use to him than almost any other natural phenomena. The fact that so many of their names originate in Greek myth – narcissus, hyacinth, daphne, not to mention the nymph Flora, herself supposed to have given the world the seeds of countless varieties – shows how potent their symbolism was, even in antiquity. In the monastic gardens of the Middle Ages, flowers were likewise seen as emblems of Christian virtues: above all the lily, whose white colour and sweet smell were associated with the purity and sanctity of the Virgin Mary; and the rose, signifying the blood of Our Saviour, just as its prickles suggested the crown of thorns. The

(Left) The rose garden at Syon Park in Middlesex. Begun in 1967, it now covers ten acres, and contains over two hundred different varieties.

Benedictines were particularly devoted to the cultivation of flowers, illustrating them as borders to their missals, and giving them characteristics such as those listed by the Catholic Henry Hawkins in his *Partheneia Sacra* of 1633: 'the *Violet* of Humilitie, the *Gilloflower* of Patience, the *Marygold* of Charitie, the *Hiacinth* of Hope, the *Sun-flower* of Contemplation.'

Cut flowers were used in interiors from an early date, particularly to obviate the smells that were rife before the invention of the water-closet, and the nosegays still carried in the Lord Mayor of London's processions are a reminder of how necessary they were outdoors as well as indoors. Many medieval flower gardens, like the one belonging to the nuns of Romsey, recorded as being accessible to outsiders as early as 1092, may thus have been run on commercial lines. The thin flower borders used to edge grass plots in the walled 'pleasure garden' were usually composed of specimen flowering plants, probably with more thought for their exoticism than for their appearance *en masse*. The 'closed knots' of clipped hedges filled with flowers of one colour carried this a stage further, but perhaps the first evidence of flowers being grouped in a painterly way comes in Sir Henry Wotton's *Elements of Architecture* (1624), describing 'the Garden of Sir *Henry Fanshaw*, at his seat in *Ware-Parke*, where I wel remember, hee did so precisely examine the *tinctures*, and *seasons* of his *flowres*, that in their *setting*, the *inwardest* of those which were to come up at the same time, should be always a little *darker* than the *outmost*, and to serve them for a kinde of gentle *shadow*, like a piece not of *Nature*, but of *Arte*.'

Scents were also considered of the greatest importance in the sixteenth and seventeenth centuries, and again they could have symbolic connotations, as we are reminded by the romantic inscription on a marquetry table-top in the High Great Chamber at Hardwick – 'The redolent smelle of eglantyne/we stagges extol to the divyne' (a reference to the stags supporting the Cavendish coat-of-arms). Francis Bacon gives whole lists of flowers whose '*Breath* . . . is farre Sweeter in the Aire . . . then in the hand,' and which were evidently intended to be planted together, in beds or borders near the house, particularly recommending 'Wall-Flowers, which are very Delightfull, to be set under a Parler, or lower Chamber window'. Honeysuckles he seems to have thought too strong, however, unless 'they be somewhat a farre off '.

The increasing interest in the natural world that characterized early-seventeenth-century thought, leading to the discoveries of Newton and the founding of the Royal

Society, encouraged the publication of 'florilegia' or catalogues of flowering plants. Dutch and Flemish botanists and engravers took the lead, with books like Crispin van de Passe's *Hortus Floridus* of 1614 illustrating types of iris and lily, narcissus and hollyhock, that are still favourite garden flowers. But it was John Parkinson's *Paradisi in Sole Paradisus Terrestris*, published in 1629 and dedicated to Queen Henrietta Maria, that was among the first to distinguish plants grown for herbal use and those 'for ornament and pleasure', suggesting they be kept apart. The age of discovery also encouraged a passion for exotic flowers from far-away places. At Henry VIII's court, the cult of the double-clove carnation, brought from Turkey via Italy and Spain, can be judged from its appearance in so many of Holbein's portraits. The 'tulipomania' of the seventeenth century is well-known, reaching a climax in England in the reign of William and Mary, though rare sports were acquired for fabulous sums before 1637. Hundreds of different varieties of anemone and ranunculus can also be found in contemporary planting lists, like those which Sir Thomas Hanmer drew up in 1638.

On the whole, the main parterre of a Baroque garden, on the central axis of the house, would be too big to be closely planted with flowers (still a very expensive commodity), though they might be planted in thin borders along the surrounding walks or terraces. The flower garden proper was more likely to be on the side of the house facing the private apartments, like Queen Mary II's 'Privy Garden' at Hampton Court. Formality was still the order of the day, and trees were often used at the centre of flower-beds or knots to give scale, and to emphasize the regularity of the design. Celia Fiennes, visiting Ingestre in Staffordshire in 1698, found 'a flower garden divided into knotts in which were 14 Cyprus trees which were grown up very tall some of them and kept cutt close in four squares down to the bottom.' It was natural that the eighteenth-century taste for 'Picturesque' gardening would be inimical to serried ranks of flowers in symmetrical layouts such as these.

Joseph Addison's famous article in *The Tatler* of April 1710, one of the early manifestos of the movement, describes his dream of a 'happy Region . . . inhabited by the Goddess of *Liberty* . . . covered with a wonderful Profusion of Flowers, that, without being disposed into regular Borders and Parterres, grew promiscuously, and had a greater beauty in their natural Luxuriancy and Disorder, than they could have received from the Checks and Restraints of Art.' Such principles were slow to be adopted, and as late as 1728, Batty Langley's *New Principles of Gardening* could claim that

'Obelisks of Trellip-Work cover'd with Passion-Flowers, Grapes, Honey-Suckles, and White Jessemine, are beautiful Ornaments in the Center of an open Plain, Flower-Garden, &c,' while Thomas Jefferson, visiting Blenheim in 1786, long after Capability Brown's work there, thought that 'art appears too much . . . every here & there small thickets of shrubs, in oval raised beds, cultivated, & flowers among the shrubs.'

Today, when only the bones of Capability Brown's layouts have survived – the great clumps of hardwoods, grown to full maturity; the serpentine lakes; the smoothly contoured hills – we tend to assume that flowers were banished altogether from the country-house garden under his influence. But nothing could be further from the truth, as his bills and accounts make clear. At Petworth, for instance, Lord Egremont paid Brown in 1757 for a vast number of flowering plants, trees and shrubs intended for the Pleasure Ground, and a similar list of entirely sweet-smelling flowers was ordered by Lord Scarsdale for the 'Long Walk' at Kedleston in 1760, planned by Robert Adam.

Attempts to incorporate flowers into natural landscape settings resulted in two important developments: the idea of the herbaceous border, pioneered by Philip Southcote's Woburn Farm, Surrey, in the late 1730s; and the adoption of asymmetrical flower-beds, with curving edges, to achieve the kind of 'carefully careless' look seen in the garden designs of Thomas Wright of Durham, and the charming watercolours of Thomas Robins. At Woburn Farm, Southcote's sandy walk round the circuit of his *ferme ornée* had a continuous flower-border on the inner side consisting mainly of hollyhock, lily, golden rod and crown imperial, with an edging of pinks at the front, and mixed shrubs including roses, syringa, sweet briar and lilac behind. The scale was carefully controlled so as to form a gradually rising bank, while on the outer side there were open views over sheep-pastures and wheatfields, comparable with Walpole's 'enamelled meadows' at Strawberry Hill.

Thomas Wright's elaborate plan for Badminton, made in 1750, included 'the Duches's Flower Garden in which is design'd a Chinees Temple wing'd with umbrellos to shade the Auricula and other curious kinds of Flowers [shown in rows of flower-pots in his accompanying sketch] . . . Borderd with Beds of Flowers and Thickets of Roses.' Rather similar island beds of irregular outline were also a feature of the famous flower-garden at Nuneham Courtenay, designed for Earl Harcourt by the poet William Mason, and commemorated in the watercolours of Paul Sandby. As Mason wrote in his somewhat tedious epic, *The English Garden* (1772-81),

So here did Art arrange her flow'ry groups
Irregular, yet not in patches quaint,
But interpos'd between the wandring lines
Of shaven turf which twisted to the path.

The old problem of incorporating flower-beds in the landscape garden without too great a feeling of artificiality was often solved in the late eighteenth century by placing them some way away from the house, either surrounded by walls or by thick woodland. The old Scottish tradition of long herbaceous borders forming a central path in the kitchen garden – discreetly hiding the rows of vegetables behind – was an answer which well satisfied the Hibernian instinct for profit and pleasure combined. Faced with the same difficulties in trying to restore flowers to the immediate surroundings of the house, Humphry Repton revived the idea of the 'flower basket', known from classical antiquity, but hardly used in England until about 1800. By their very obvious artificiality, he intended these to act as 'furnishings' in the landscape rather than integral parts of the layout – just as the informal Regency serving-tables, jardinières and fortepianos that had begun to clutter the rooms inside the house were not held to interfere with their architectural settings. John Adey Repton, Humphry's son and successor, designed very large 'Hardenberg baskets' for Blickling and Gunton in Norfolk, giving the illusion of having bottoms, and with sides of interwoven metal strands resembling rope-mouldings that came into fashion after the Battle of Trafalgar.

The invention of the sealed glass 'Wardian case', which enabled the tenderest plants to survive long sea voyages, immensely widened the gardener's palette in the early nineteenth century, and a taste for the lurid colours of tropical blooms can be paralleled in the Victorian stained glass of Hardman and Kemp, and the painted decoration of J. G. Crace. The first dahlia had arrived from Mexico in 1789, but it was not until 1842, for instance, that Robert Fortune introduced forty cultivars of peony, brought from China. Vast hothouses now also made it possible for the head-gardener of a great country house to provide colour all the year round. John Fleming, the Duke of Sutherland's gardener at Cliveden from 1849, is said to have re-bedded the whole of the great parterre below the house one night so that Queen Victoria, who was staying, could wake up to an entirely different colour scheme next morning. Such huge formal gardens (and the Sutherlands had two more, equally big, at Trentham and Dunrobin) were thought at the time to revive the principles of seventeenth-century formal gardening, though the predominance of annuals or dwarf succulents arranged by colour in large geometrical blocks actually produced a very different effect – surviving in debased form in many of our public parks.

The aesthetic reaction against such an obvious use of brilliant colour, very often out of key with the mellow red brick or soft Bath stone of an old country house, came initially from the Arts and Crafts school, though French theorists were also a major influence. John Lindley was the first to invoke the 'law of simultaneous contrasts' worked out by Michel Eugène Chevreul, chemist and director of the Gobelins factory, who advocated the use of complementary colours and graded sequences of 'warm' and 'cold' tones. These views, not without influence on the later Impressionist painters, were fiercely opposed by Donald Beaton, famous for his polychrome flower-beds at Shrubland Park in Suffolk, set against Sir Charles Barry's formal Italianate terraces – but were to be revived at the end of the century by the redoubtable Gertrude Jekyll. Miss Jekyll was also a close friend of the watercolourist Hercules Brabazon, praised by Ruskin as 'the only person since Turner at whose feet I can sit and worship and learn about colour', and her revival of the herbaceous border as one of the key components of the garden was conceived in painterly as well as scientific terms.

Some of the most celebrated features of twentieth-century gardens, like Laurence Johnston's red borders at Hidcote, and V. Sackville-West's White Garden at Sissing-hurst, owe their inspiration to Gertrude Jekyll's keen sense of the flower garden as a work of art where restraint is often more telling than bold display: thus in *Colour Scheme in the Flower Garden*, published in 1908, and perhaps her most influential book, she writes 'white flowers are the only ones that possess the advantage of heightening the tone of flowers which have only a light tint of colour'; 'grey helps all the colours gain in purity and brilliance'; and 'any experienced colourist knows that the blues will be more telling – more purely blue – by the juxtaposition of rightly placed complementary colour.' Another of her achievements was to distil the essence of traditional English cottage gardens, applying their principles to the larger scale of the country house.

Many of her *dicta* – that flowers which bloom at the same time should be placed near each other, or that earth should never be visible in a flower-bed (at least in the summer) – are still with us, and the mixture of herbs and ground-cover plants with the more conventional inhabitants of the herbaceous border might also have appealed to her in an age less well endowed with gardeners and handymen, and more dependent on the efforts of the châtelaine and her secateurs.

The scent of roses drifts through an open door at Haddon Hall in Derbyshire, its stone steps worn by generations of Vernons and Manners, and their guests.

*T*he Lupin Garden at Chatsworth, planted recently on part of the site of Paxton's Great Conservatory.
*(Right) The celebrated White Garden at Sissinghurst, created by V. Sackville-West in the 1930s, and inspired
by some of Gertrude Jekyll's earlier theories on the use of colour.*

A yellow border at Great Dixter in Sussex (above), complementing the rose-red brick and tiled roofs of old barns and oast-houses. (Below) A bold planting of tulips and forget-me-nots at Nymans, in the same county. (Left) Yellow and red flowers grouped in the sunken garden at Packwood House, Warwickshire, created in the 1930s by Graham Baron Ash.

*W*ide herbaceous borders flanking a narrow path at Crathes Castle, Kincardineshire (left). Gardens
like these fulfil Gertrude Jekyll's dictum that earth should never be visible in a flower-bed – except in winter.
(Above) A border at Dyrham Park in Gloucestershire showing a mixture of herbs and herbaceous plants, with
a controlled colour scheme of silver-grey foliage and soft pink flowers.

VI

STATUES, URNS AND VASES

The humanism of the Italian Renaissance – the setting of man at the centre of an ordered universe – received one of its clearest expressions in the idea of the sculpture garden, where nature was not only tamed but also dominated by representations of the human form. Bramante's Belvedere Court at the Vatican, begun about 1505 for Pope Julius II, was perhaps the first to revive the idea, its use of excavated Greek and Roman statues emphasizing the link with the gardens of classical antiquity, and illustrating the Arcadian visions of Virgil, or the empathy between living forms found in Ovid's *Metamorphoses*. Gardens of the early English Renaissance were more likely to be furnished with heraldic imagery, like the painted wooden statues of the King's Beasts

One of a pair of stone vases carved with pan-pipes and goat's masks at Wimpole, Cambridgeshire. (Right) Lead putti and vases alternate on the terrace at Wilton House, near Salisbury.

at Henry VIII's Hampton Court. But a number of columns and obelisks from the garden at Nonsuch are illustrated in the famous Lumley Inventory of 1590, and their brightly coloured marbles suggest that some at least may have been brought back from Lord Lumley's embassy to Florence in the 1570s.

The first true sculpture garden in England was the creation of Lord Lumley's great-nephew, the Earl of Arundel, who took Inigo Jones to Italy, and who acquired there the first important collection of classical antiquities to reach these shores. While some of the finest statues were displayed in a sculpture gallery overlooking the Thames at Arundel House, others were arranged on plinths and balustrades in the raised parterre between the house and the Strand – as depicted in the background of the Earl's portrait, now at Welbeck. Francis Bacon, who felt that 'Statua's, and such Things' added 'State, and Magnificence, but nothing to the true Pleasure of a Garden', was presumably being sarcastic when he visited Arundel House and 'coming into the . . . Garden, where there were a great number of Ancient Statues of naked Men and Women, made a stand, and as astonish'd cryed out: *The Resurrection*.' On the other hand, Charles I was so struck by the idea that he sent Hubert le Sueur to Rome to take moulds of the most famous classical sculptures for the gardens at St James's, while Nicholas Stone's rather lumpish statues of Venus and Cupid, Diana and other deities, which still survive at Wilton, show how native sculptors were quick to take up the theme.

Just as the Elizabethan and Stuart parterre was often conceived as the setting for court masques, so its statues could be seen as actors, enhancing the associational value of the garden. Perhaps the best example of this is Sir John Danvers' garden at Chelsea, begun in 1622, whose scheme has been interpreted by Roy Strong as an evocation of Arcadia, very much in tune with Samuel Daniel's masques for Anne of Denmark, the *Queens Arcadia* (1605) and *Hymen's Triumph* (1614). The sphinxes guarding the main entrance to the garden symbolized the search for ancient wisdom, while the flanking statues of Cain and Abel, and Hercules and Antaeus, represented the search for lost innocence before man's fall, and the defeat of earthly passions – the one biblical, the other classical. Then in the garden itself Aubrey described statues (again by Nicholas Stone) depicting 'the Faithful Shepherd, and the Faithfull Shepherdesse . . . expressing Love-passions in the very freestone: where you read rustick beauty mixt with antique innocent simplicitie.' Again the inspiration for such complex imagery probably came from Italy, and it is interesting to find John Evelyn visiting the Palazzo Negrone at Genoa in 1644 and finding 'a grove of stately trees, furnish'd with artificial

Sheepe, Shepheards, & Wild Beasts, so naturaly cut in a grey-stone . . . [that] you would imagine yourselfe in a Wildernesse & Silent Country, side-ways in the heart of a great Citty.'

Evelyn's travel diaries of the 1640s show his particular excitement at the amount of statuary in French and Italian gardens, drawing lessons for its display in the harsher English climate. Thus the 'incomparable statues' in the Belvedere Court 'are for defence against the Weather shut up in their Neeches with dores of Wainscot', while at the Villa Medici on the Pincian Hill, 'here is also a row balustr'd with white marble, on which are erected divers statues and heads, covered over with the natural shrubbs, Ivys & other perennial Greenes, as in nices.' The disintegration of stone and marble outdoors was a perennial problem, however, and it was partly for this reason that lead-work became so popular in the late seventeenth century. The whole point of statues, according to John Woolridge writing in 1677, was for 'Winter diversion . . . to re-compence the loss of past pleasures, and to buoy up hope of another Spring,' so the boxing-in practised in colder countries like Russia from an early date was rarely fol-lowed in England.

Large numbers of lead figures by Jan Van Nost and his successor, Andries Carpen-tière, survive in English country-house gardens, but their weathered and lichened appearance which we have come to admire is very different from the sculptors' orig-inal intention. Seventeenth- and eighteenth-century accounts invariably record their being painted to resemble stone or marble, brass or bronze, or even in polychrome. A visitor to John Cheere's famous statuary yard at Hyde Park Corner in the 1750s described the figures 'cast in lead as large as life and frequently painted with an inten-tion to resemble nature. They consisted of Punch, Harlequin, Columbine and other pantomimical figures; mowers whetting their scythes, haymakers resting on their rakes, gamekeepers in the act of shooting and Roman soldiers with firelocks, but above all that of an African, kneeling with a sundial on his head.' The lead slave trade was evidently brisk, for a number of examples of the blackamoor sundial still exists, many of them bearing traces of red, green and yellow paint on their feathered skirts and head-dresses.

The sundial had been thought an appropriate ornament for the garden since at least the beginning of the sixteenth century, Brise Augustyn of Westminster supply-ing no less than twenty for Hampton Court in June 1534. The demonstration of sci-ence, as in the automata of Salomon de Caus's grottoes, or the orrery on a column recommended by John Woolridge, was one aspect of its popularity, but its emblematic value was still more powerful. The garden, with its cycle of seasons, was a constant reminder of the transitory nature of man's existence:

> As Time and Howres paseth awaye
> So doeth the life of man decaye
> As Time can be redeemed with no cost
> Bestow it well and let no houre be lost.

Pillars too were looked on as symbolic and appropriate ornaments, representing justice and strength of purpose. The large column in the centre of the Great Garden at Wimbledon was erected in the 1590s, probably in conscious tribute to the crowned pillar device of Elizabeth I, while another in porphyry seen at Wilton by Daniel Defoe, and 32 feet high, was used to support a marble statue of Venus.

Very precise instructions as to the placing of the different deities can be found in eighteenth-century treatises on gardening. As Stephen Switzer put it, in his *Ichnographia Rustica* in 1718, 'it cann't but be an unpleasant Sight . . . to view *Jupiter*, *Mars*, *Neptune*, and the rest of the capital Deities of Heaven, misplac'd, and by a meanness of spirit below a good Designer, set perching upon a little Pedestal; one like a Citizen; a second with a Pike in his Hand, like a Foot-Soldier; and the third upon dry Land with a Trident, like a Cart-filler.' Batty Langley's *New Principles of Gardening*, published ten years later, gives detailed lists of the figures suitable for different locations, descending to some of the lower slopes of Olympus for inspiration: thus Flora and Cloris might be attended in the flower garden by '*Runcina* the Goddess of Weeding'; Diana and Actaeon could be accompanied in 'Woods and Groves' by Philomela who was transformed into a nightingale, and Itis who became a pheasant; while 'small Inclosures of Wheat, Barley, &c. in a Wilderness' might suit '*Robigus* a God who preserved Corn from being blasted . . . and *Tutelina* a Goddess, who had the Tuition of Corn in the Fields.'

Garden statues could also convey a political message. At Stowe, Rysbrack's series of the Saxon gods and goddesses who gave their name to the days of the week recalled the 'ancient liberties' of druidical Britain, in the same way as his busts for the Temple of British Worthies, including King Alfred and the Black Prince, gave an illustrious pedigree to Lord Cobham's brand of patriotic Whiggery. As the taste for 'Picturesque' gardening grew, however, statues began to be thought too artificial as ornaments for a purely landscape setting, and urns or vases were preferred. In William Shenstone's words, 'Urns are more solemn, if large and plain; more beautiful, if less and ornamented. Solemnity is perhaps their print, and the situation of them should still cooperate with it.' Orange and bay trees placed outdoors in the summer had in the seventeenth century been placed in gilded lead or blue-and-white China or Delft vases, as can be seen in the famous Stoke Edith needlework hangings – or in painted Versailles tubs, which would take larger specimens, as in Peter Rysbrack's painting of the Orange Tree Garden at Chiswick. But these too were considered gaudy, and out of key with the muted colours of nature, by Capability Brown's day.

Chaste neo-classical urns made of Coade stone and based on celebrated antique prototypes, like the Warwick Vase, were thought more suitable incidents on the serpentine walks of *fermes ornées* like Shenstone's own at the Leasowes. Latin inscriptions and dedications invoked the world of Homer and Virgil, and urns were dedicated to the memory of friends to provide a tinge of pleasing melancholy. At Shugborough, the Shepherds Monument consisted of a bas-relief by Scheemakers after Poussin's famous *Et in Arcadia Ego*, one of the most potent images of the 'Picturesque' movement, breathing the same air of mystery that haunts Keats' 'Ode to a Grecian Urn'.

Repton's restoration of the terrace as a podium for the house in the early years of the nineteenth century also restored the fashion for statues and vases – filled with trailing plants in the Italian manner – lining stone or terracotta balustrades. Matthew Digby Wyatt's new formal gardens at Castle Ashby, dating from the 1840s, were bounded by balustrades inspired by the Jacobean lettering round the parapet of the house – but instead of the psalms in Latin, somewhat gloomy quotations in English from the Song of Solomon (including 'The grass withereth and fadeth away . . .') were rendered in four-foot-high terracotta letters. A revival of interest in the gardens of the Italian Renaissance persuaded William Waldorf Astor at the end of the century to acquire the famous balustrade from the forecourt of the Villa Borghese in Rome, though the authorities prevented him from acquiring the antique statues that stood on it. When the balustrade was re-erected below the terrace at Cliveden in the 1890s, it was thus crowned with a pair of handmaidens of Diana, carved by Poirier and Cayot for Louis XIV's Marly – not perhaps correct from a purist point of view but splendid in scale and in their picturesque effect. Both at Cliveden and at Hever Castle, which he acquired in 1906, Astor's Roman sarcophagi placed against dark yew hedges, stone urns silhouetted against the sky, and use of statues to emphasize the perspective of a long vista, can be compared with the work of Harold Peto at Buscot or Achille

Duchêne at Blenheim; a mixture of formality with romantic yearning that can also be found at the turn of the century in illustrated books on French and Italian gardens.

One of the most remarkable collections of English garden sculpture is that at Anglesey Abbey, in the garden which the first Lord Fairhaven began to lay out in 1926, on an unpromising stretch of flat Cambridgeshire fen. Rysbrack's *Father Time* supporting a sundial in the centre of the Herbaceous Garden, the ten Corinthian columns from Chesterfield House set round the circular Temple Lawn, or the six Coade stone caryatids from Soane's Bank of England marking the cross-axis in the Great Avenue to a large extent dictate the form of their new settings, and can be compared with the antique furniture collected for neo-Georgian interiors in the 1930s. Since the War a few notable attempts have been made to create gardens round contemporary sculpture – as at Sutton Place, where the Ben Nicholson 'wall', a huge white marble relief, is mirrored in a formal lily pond designed by Sir Geoffrey Jellicoe. But far the most successful synthesis between art and nature has been achieved at Glenkiln in Dumfriesshire, where Henry Moore's King and Queen (among other sculptures) gaze majestically over a Scottish grouse moor – not perhaps a garden in the accepted sense, but a return to the 'Picturesque', and to Burke's ideals of the Beautiful and the Sublime.

The sundial at Drummond Castle, carved in 1630 by John Mylne, Master Mason to Charles I. (Right) Van Nost's lead shepherd boy at Canons Ashby in Northamptonshire.

A maenad playing a syrinx, and wearing a sheep's pelt, announces pagan pleasures in the garden at Anglesey Abbey, Cambridgeshire, while (left) a satyr beckons towards the woods in Kent's Vale of Venus at Rousham. Great care was taken in the eighteenth century to place statues of classical deities in appropriate settings.

A garden bestiary: (above) the Wild Boar at Castle Howard, a lead copy of the famous antique statue in the Uffizi, plays host to visiting peacocks; (below left) a monkey, supporting Van Nost's giant Vase of the Seasons at Melbourne in Derbyshire; and (below right) a sacred cow, in the Chinese garden at Biddulph Grange, Staffordshire. (Left) one of a pair of kneeling slaves at Melbourne, also by Van Nost, supplied in 1700 at a cost of £30.

*E*dwardian opulence: antique terracotta jars at Hever Castle, brought back from the Middle East
by William Waldorf Astor, and (left) Italian copies of Greek and Roman statues in the 9th Duke of Marlborough's
Water Garden at Blenheim Palace. The sphinx is said to have been modelled with the features (and
the long neck) of his wife, the American heiress, Consuelo Vanderbilt.

*Sculpture as a focal point: (above) one of a number of
sundials telling the passing of the hours in the garden at Penshurst in Kent;
(below) the Byzantine urn in the Sunk Garden at Nymans; and
(right) a copy of the Belvedere Antinous in the centre of the parterre at
Penshurst – a souvenir of Italy among the orchards of the Weald.*

VII

ALLEES AND VISTAS

The difference between the *allée* and the avenue (both words of French derivation) is one of scale, but also implies a different use: the former, a walk within the garden proper; the latter, a drive in the park beyond. In the French formal garden, the *allées*, bordered by pollarded trees, clipped hedges or simply lawns, constitute the framework of the layout – as with the streets of one of Vauban's fortified towns, or the city plans devised by Baroque architects like Bernini earlier in the seventeenth century.

The larger enclosed gardens of the Middle Ages, square or oblong in shape, often had perimeter paths of sand and gravel protected by a 'cloister' or tunnel-arbour built on wooden rods or

(Above) A giant urn silhouetted against the sky closes a vista at Chatsworth.
(Left) The laburnum walk at Bodnant, supported on a metal pergola frame.

101

withies and covered with roses, vines and ivy. These were intended to provide a walk in the shade, particularly for the ladies of the household at a time when the sexes were still very much separated in and outside the house, and when the palest complexions were also highly prized. In the early seventeenth century, Francis Bacon still recommends 'a Covert Alley, upon Carpenters Worke, about Twelve Foot in Height, by which you may goe in Shade, into the *Garden*' – and others framed 'likewise for Shelter, that when the Wind blows Sharpe, you may walke, as in a Gallery.'

The idea of the *allée* as an outdoor Long Gallery for exercise and conversation in fine weather can be confirmed by the number of such rooms whose barrel-vaulted ceilings are conversely decorated with plasterwork trellises of flowers, leaves and branches – a tradition carried right up to the twentieth century with Oliver Messel's trailing vines painted on the ceiling of the long gallery at Parham. Pleached lime trees were particularly favoured for walks from the sixteenth century 'for both shade and sweetness', as John Aubrey put it in his description of the Earl of Exeter's garden at Wimbledon. The scent of limes was balanced by their tendency to drop a black sticky honeydew on the innocent promenader, however, and other species such as beech and hornbeam also became popular – the former because it kept its leaf through the winter and helped preserve the 'architecture' of the garden from one season to another. Yew was of course even better for this purpose, and the tunnel of yew at Melbourne Hall in Derbyshire, planted by the Royal gardeners London and Wise about 1704 is – at just over 290 feet – thought to be the longest in Europe.

D'Argenville's *Theory and Practice of Gardening*, translated by John James in 1712, characterizes the different 'Palisades' or hedges lining an *allée* in highly architectural terms, 'making as it were a green Wall or green Tapestry'. The tallest, cut with the help of 'tall double Ladders and Rolling Carriages', he calls 'Fans and Curtains . . . which serve to stop the Sight, to shut up Places that are disagreeable, or to sever the parts of a Garden,' while 'those we call *Banquettes*, they are low Palisades Breast-high, ordinarily not exceeding 3 or 4 Foot.' Those most commonly found nowadays, clipped like boxes supported on stilt-like trunks – as in the stilt garden at Hidcote, or flanking the south garden at Chatsworth – he calls 'à l'Italienne', while the most elaborate of all 'cut into Arches', with 'Balls or Vases . . . formed by Shoots of Horn-beam . . . on the Head of each Peer . . . a Kind of Order of Rural Architecture.'

Elms were also used for the larger *allée*, such as the gigantic *patte-d'oie* or goose-foot pattern of three avenues radiating from a double semicircle of trees which was planted at Greenwich soon after the Restoration, probably following an original design by Le Nôtre. Though the great French garden designer never visited England, his influence was strongly felt, particularly after his master Claude Mollet's son, André, entered the service of Charles II. However, the idea of the 'limitless vista', created with ease in the flat landscape surrounding Versailles, was not so easily achieved among the highly compartmented small-holdings of Holland or the hilly countryside of much of Britain – and sometimes the effect had to be gained by painted 'Perspectives' or *trompes-l'oeil*, seeming to extend the vista into infinity. John Evelyn, who visited Saint-Germain in 1644, recorded that 'in the uper Walkes are two Perspectives very pretty ones, seeming to enlarge the allys,' and the painter Jacques Rousseau who worked in both France and England became a specialist in this field in the 1680s and '90s. D'Argenville describes a variation on the form with a false grotto opening, but calls such 'Perspective Works . . . now but little in use.'

The straight walk reached its apogee in the early eighteenth century, with elaborate stars of radiating vistas like those seen in Peter Rysbrack's paintings of Chiswick, or Balthasar Nebot's of Hartwell: each one aligned on a pavilion, an obelisk, a pillar, or an already existing 'object' at some distance. John Aislabie's principal avenue at Studley Royal was aligned on the towers of Ripon Minster; one of the Earl of Mar's *allées* at Alloa took in Stirling Castle, and another the Palace of Elphinstone; while at Easton Neston, Lord Lempster added a spire to the neighbouring church of Greens Norton, not out of solicitude for the parishioners or for the glory of God, but so that it would act as an 'eyecatcher' for one of his two principal vistas.

Many houses like Easton Neston, Erddig and Wimpole had a gallery on the upper floor running from front to back of the house on the central axis, offering views of several miles in each direction. Celia Fiennes, describing Ingestre in Staffordshire, records that 'the vista is quite through the house and so to the gardens and through a long walke of trees of a mile through the parke to a lodge or summer house at the end, which lookes very finely, it being a riseing ground up to the parke.'

Stephen Switzer was one of the first to express disquiet at the prevalence of the straight *allée* in his *Ichnographia Rustica* of 1718: '. . . tho' a few of these Walks are absolutely necessary, in Respect to the Grandeur and general Beauty of a Situation, as the Middle and Side Walk, and a very few Diagonals, yet it is an unpardonable Fault . . . to have scarce any Thing in a whole Design, but carries open Walks; so that . . . one shall scarce find any private or natural Turn in the Whole.' By contrast, he cites 'that beautiful Wood belonging to the Earl of *Carlisle*, at *Castle-Howard*, where Mr London design'd a Star, which would have Spoil'd the Wood; but that his Lordship's superlative Genius prevented it, and to the great Advancement of the Design, has given it that Labyrinth diverting Model we now see it.'

The privacy of 'solitary walks' like those in Wray Wood may seem a curious concept today, but the numbers of people attached to a noble household at the time meant that it would be difficult to see the length of a vista unencumbered by fellow humans. The garden as a place where man could commune with nature, already foreshadowed by the melancholy Elizabethan seeking 'the shade of the Greenwood tree', gained ground with the Natural Landscape movement. At the same time, writers like William Shenstone underlined the boredom of the long straight walk, compared with the serpentine path, revealing new Claudian 'pictures' at every turn: 'to move on continually and find no change of scene in the least attendant on our change of place, must give actual pain to a person of taste. For such an one to be condemned to pass along the famous vista from Moscow to Petersburg, or that other from Agra to Lahor in India, must be as disagreeable a sentence as to be condemned to labour at the gallies. I conceived some idea of the sensation he must feel, from walking but a few minutes, immured, betwixt Lord D—'s high-shorn yew-hedges; which run exactly parallel, at the distance of about ten feet; and are contrived perfectly to exclude all kind of objects whatsoever.'

Capability Brown's idea of a serpentine walk forming a circuit of the 'Pleasure Ground', either for walking or for driving in a pony trap, offered a very different kind of experience, although the viewpoints on the way were often contrived with just as much artifice. In the same way as it had become the common practice to taper a short avenue or *allée* so that it appeared longer than it was, Shenstone recommended a vista to be 'widened in front, and planted there with ewe trees, then firs, then with trees more and more shady, till they end in the almond-willow, or silver osier . . . which deception will be encreased, if the nearer dark trees, are proportionable and truly larger than those at the end.' Joseph Spence was also fully aware of the importance of perspective in 'composing' a picturesque view, and two of his 'general rules' about landscape design, written in the form of a letter to the Rev Mr Wheeler in 1751, propose how 'to make objects that are too near seem farther off: which is done by shewing more of the intermediate ground and narrowing your view to them more and more as it recedes from you;' while 'to draw distant objects nearer to you and make them seem part of your work . . . is done by hiding the intermediate length of ground and planting what may fall and unite, to the eye, with such distant objects.'

A garden building, or even the house itself, could provide such an 'object', varying greatly in appearance from whatever angle it was viewed. Thus the critical Polyphon in William Gilpin's *Dialogue upon the Gardens . . . at Stow* (1748), was finally persuaded to 'run out into the highest Encomiums of the many beautiful Terminations of the several Walks and Vistas; and observe how many Uses each Object served . . . "For Instance, says he, the pavilion you shewed me from the Temple of Venus, terminates that Terrace in a very grand Manner . . . Yet the same Building . . . view'd thro' a retired Vista, can take upon it the lowly Form of a close Retreat." '

The return of formal gardening in the nineteenth century brought with it a new appreciation of the straight vista, often arranged with steps so as to provide a higher vanishing-point, and thus an impression of greater length. At Biddulph Grange, the flights are arranged some way away from each other, but from the terrace in front of the house 'read' as one continuous stair of monumental proportions. The walk itself is lined with rhododendrons, first used for such a purpose by Capability Brown at Kew, and later increasingly popular planted under a canopy of taller trees. Other exotic shrubs like azaleas, Japanese maples and liquidambars gave colour to long woodland or valley walks, though there is the sad story of a whole walk of *Rhododendron campbelliae* being planted at Belvoir, without realizing that it would take fifteen years to flower – and being cut down in despair after fourteen years of patient waiting.

Towards the end of the century, the pergola walk came back into its own, reviving the old sixteenth-century idea of the tunnel-arbour but giving it a more architectural emphasis in keeping with the material used for the house, whether brick, stone or timber. Harold Peto's feeling for Italian Renaissance gardens led to pergolas of Doric or Ionic columns covered with vines, while Jekyll and Lutyens were content with the farmhouse character of rough-hewn stone or chalk pillars, supporting lichened oak beams, and covered with clematis and climbing roses. Thin metal pergola frames, first developed in Germany, were also used as a practically invisible support for tunnels of wisteria or laburnum – as at Bodnant – allowing the long clusters of flowers to hang down like bunches of grapes from a vine. At a time when country-house gardens are again being viewed as a series of 'outdoor rooms', these *allées* are reminders of the sixteenth-century long gallery or the seventeenth-century enfilade, though with a sense of controlled colour that owes much to twentieth-century interior decoration.

*P*ollarded limes in the French style lead to a flowery meadow at Cranborne Manor, Dorset.
*(Left) The Ring Pond at Chatsworth, with the beech allée beyond, leading to a colossal bust of the
6th Duke of Devonshire, on a column made of blocks of marble from the Temple of Minerva Sunias. The serpentine
hedge was only eighteen inches high when it was planted in 1953, inspired by the 'crinkle-crankle' walls
sometimes found in old kitchen gardens, whose south-facing bays protected the tenderer plants.*

*T*he yew tunnel at Melbourne in Derbyshire, planted by
the Royal gardeners, George London and Henry Wise, about 1704 and – at
just over 290 feet – thought to be the longest in Europe.
(Right) One of the chestnut avenues at Anglesey Abbey, Cambridgeshire,
forming a cross-axis with the Great Avenue, planted to
commemorate the coronation of King George VI. The vast urn is one of
a pair, originally from Stafford House in London.

*T̲wo hornbeam allées planted by Lawrence Johnston at Hidcote in Gloucestershire:
(above) the Long Walk, with its clipped hedges, given scale by the huge Monterey pine on the right;
(right) the Stilt Garden with its pleached 'boxes' – or 'palissades à l'Italienne' – supported
on trimmed trunks. As V. Sackville-West wrote, 'it gives a sudden little touch of France to this very
English garden'. The wrought-iron gate in the distance, flanked by evergreen oaks, frames
a wide view of the Cotswolds.*

*V*istas prolonged by steps: (above) the long walk at Biddulph Grange, Cheshire, with flights placed at long intervals, but looking like a continuous staircase seen from the terrace of the house; (below) pots of marguerites guarding a brick stair at Sissinghurst; and (right) the axial walk at Knightshayes, parallel with the house. The steps and flanking stone figures mark the transition from formal to wild garden.

VIII

HERB AND KITCHEN GARDENS

The medicinal value of plants was one of the principal motives for gardening in the early Middle Ages, particularly among the monastic orders, which maintained physic gardens or herbariums on a large scale. However, the separation of utilitarian from decorative species was already a feature of Greek gardens in the first millennium BC, and the excavations at Pompeii show that the Romans had developed a thriving kitchen-garden tradition, which they brought north to the outer limits of the empire. Thus the elder Pliny's *Naturalis Historia* lists at least twelve different types of cabbage and kale, eleven types of lettuce, and numerous members of the onion family, while the Roman villa at Fishbourne in Sussex had a vegetable garden between its north and west wings, within easy range of the kitchen quarters.

(Above) The Herb Garden at Hardwick in Derbyshire, using mostly plants known before 1700. (Left) Fruit trees in blossom in the orchards at Penshurst Place, Kent.

The first English books on horticulture were largely devoted to the growing of vines, herbs and vegetables, like 'The Feate of Gardening' written in the 1330s by John Standerwyk, probably chief gardener to Edward III, which has long sections on the onion tribe, colewort, parsley and saffron, or the herbals of Friar Henry Daniel introducing rosemary (which had come to England with Queen Philippa of Hainault in 1340), and other foreign plants like germander and sweet marjoram, pomegranates and gourds. Gerard's *Herball* of 1597, perhaps the best-known and best-loved of all, was based on his experience as Lord Burghley's gardener at Theobalds and as curator of the garden kept by the College of Physicians in the City of London. His catalogue of his own garden at Holborn, published in 1596, includes the first printed reference to the potato, and the *Herball* was to influence and encourage botanists up to the time of Sir Joseph Banks.

Although the walled kitchen garden was conceived early on as a separate enclosure, herbs were often placed in the open knots of the Tudor and Stuart parterre. Gervase Markham in his essay 'Of Gardens' (1625) supposes the patterns to be set out in lines of rosemary, thyme or hyssop, and Bacon tells us that 'those which *Perfume* the Aire most delightfully, not *passed by* as the rest, but being *Trodon Upon* and *Crushed*, are Three: That is Burnet, Wilde-Time, and Water-Mints. Therefore, you are to set whole Allies of them to have the Pleasure, when you walke or tread.' At Sir John Danvers' house at Chelsea, the wide gravel walks nearest the house were bordered with hyssop backed by more than twenty-four varieties of thyme, and Aubrey records that 'Sir John was wont in fine faire mornings in the Summer to brush his Bever hatt on the Hysop and Thyme, which did perfume it with its naturall Essence: and would last a morning or longer.' Both fresh and dried herbs were also strewn on the floors of houses at this time to combat the less salubrious smells of a pre-sanitary age – just as they can be seen scattered in the path of Venus or Flora in Renaissance paintings.

Few Jacobean gardens were complete without vineyards or orchards. England had been so renowned for its dry white wines in the Middle Ages that they were exported in quantities to the Continent, and although the dissolution of the monasteries put paid to many of the finest growths, terraced vineyards were laid out on south-facing slopes at least as far north as the Trent. Robert Cecil's walled vineyard at Hatfield still survives, and his brother Lord Exeter had an equally large one in his garden at Wimbledon, drawn by Robert Smythson in 1609. John Rose, Charles II's gardener who appears in the famous picture attributed to Danckerts presenting the king with the first pineapple grown in England, was also the author of *The English Vineyard Vindicated*, published as an appendix to John Evelyn's *The French Gardiner* in 1669. Thomas Fairchild had more than fifty different varieties of grapes at his nursery at Hoxton in the 1720s, while his fruit garden was described by a contemporary as 'the greatest collection of fruits I have yet seen, and so regularly disposed . . . that I do not know any person in Europe to excel him in that particular.'

Orchards were planted not just for their practical use, but also for their beauty – the *viridarium* or *virgultum* of medieval Latin being distinguished in this sense from the more utilitarian *pomarium*. At Wimbledon in 1609 a huge area beyond the vineyard was described as 'a great Orcharde wth walkes nowe in plantinge' in 1609, while two other long rectangular orchards lay nearer the house, one with 'frute trese and roses sett amongst them'. These overlooked four large plots called 'Gardens for Earbes', conveniently placed next to the service wing of the house, only a few yards from the kitchen.

The English kitchen garden may never have reached the elaboration of Villandry or the *potager du roi* at Versailles, created by Louis XIV's gardener, Jean de La Quintinie. But the great man visited England twice, and his encyclopedic *Instructions pour les jardins fruitiers et potagers* was not only translated as *The Compleat Gard'ner* by John Evelyn in 1693, but also re-published in an abridged edition by London and Wise in 1699. One of La Quintinie's tasks was to produce vast quantities of cut flowers for the interior of Versailles, arranged in great tureens or Delft pots like those seen in the flower-pieces of Jean-Baptiste Monnoyer. His idea of cutting borders within the kitchen garden was thus as influential as his methods of forcing bulbs in greenhouses.

By the early eighteenth century, vegetables, fruit trees and herbs were generally being tidied away to a walled kitchen garden at some distance from the main parterre – although Kip's bird's-eye views often show espaliered apples, pears and plums trained on prominent boundary walls or terraces, and Pope's list of absurd topiary (from the *Guardian* article of 1713) still contains 'a Lavender Pig with Sage growing in his Belly', evidently intended for a formal herb garden near the house. The advantages of the walled garden were many. First of all it provided shelter from the worst of the weather, and a microclimate much more suitable for exotic fruits than the exposed parterres round the house. The invention of 'hot walls', heated by means of flues set into the brickwork connected to small charcoal stoves, also protected the tenderer species from frost, and anticipated the hothouses of the nineteenth century. The high walls were also useful in keeping out vermin like barking deer and rabbits, as well as in screening the necessary formality of bean-rows and onion-sets, fruit-bushes and aspa-ragus-beds, from the increasing informality of the rest of the layout.

The continual labour that was another feature of the kitchen garden was also con-sidered best out of sight at a time when servants were becoming less conspicuous in the running of the household. In the 1770s Sir Henry Harpur of Calke Abbey in Der-byshire went so far as to build a tunnel for his servants to reach the kitchen garden from their quarters in the house, without being seen from the east front. On other estates the kitchen garden was specially placed next to the stables and dovecote so that manure could be regularly spread over the beds, while a central pond collecting the rainwater from the roofs nearby ensured an adequate supply of softened water in dry spells. Some of these walled gardens were of immense size: the one at Blenheim, laid out by Vanbrugh and Henry Wise in 1705, with bastions echoing the military theme of the main parterre, had walls 14 feet high and was over 12 acres in extent. Ten years later the architect could justifiably call it the finest in Europe: 'the Kitchen Garden now the trees are in full vigour and full of fruit is really an astonishing sight. All I ever saw in England or abroad of the kind are trifles to it.'

Such Baroque splendour was not to suit the smaller Palladian villas of the following half-century, and Addison pointed the way to the very different world of the *ferme ornée* in one of his *Spectator* articles of 1712. As a 'Humorist in Gardening', he describes his own layout as 'a Confusion of Kitchin and Parterre, Orchard and Flower Garden . . . [for] I have always thought a Kitchin-Gardin a more pleasant Sight, than the finest Orangerie, or artificial Green-house . . . and am more pleased to survey my Rows of Colworts and Cabbages, with a thousand nameless Pot-herbs, springing up in their full Fragrancy and Verdure, than to see the tender Plants of Foreign Countries kept alive by artificial Heats.' Thomas Jefferson, on his tour of England in 1786, saw the archetypal English *ferme ornée* laid out by Philip Southcote at Woburn Farm in Surrey, reporting that there were '4. People [i.e. labourers] to the farm. 4. to the pleasure gar-den. 4. to the kitchen garden. all are intermixed, the pleasure garden being merely a highly ornamented walk through & round the divisions of the farm & kitchen garden.'

Experiments along these lines were too radical for most country-house owners, however. Palladio's original villas on the Brenta may have been working farms with vineyards, olive orchards and wheatfields around them, but the English *milord* wished to show himself above mere commerce. The scenes round his house were to match the pictures on the walls inside, expressing his classical education with their references to Virgil and Homer, his botanical interests with their rare trees and shrubs, and to a certain extent his agricultural expertise with their sheep and cattle. However, productive crops were rarely thought worthy of a gentleman's park and even down-to-earth farmers like Coke of Norfolk and his neighbour 'Turnip' Townshend would no more have cultivated the smooth green slopes of their parks at Holkham and Raynham than planted a formal *potager* on the main axis of the house.

On the other hand, the sweeping-away of flowers and topiary from the environs of the house in the late eighteenth century was to benefit the walled garden, and paradoxically make it less purely utilitarian. Wide cutting-borders, often flanking the central path, backed by espalier apples or pears, gave it a decorative and still formal aspect long after the rest of the estate had been 'naturalized' by the ingenious Mr Brown or one of his followers. Here the ladies of the house would repair to gather nosegays or rose-petals for pot-pourri, catch butterflies, press leaves, or sketch botanical specimens; here too they could pick the first peaches, figs and bunches of grapes from the greenhouses.

Above all, old-fashioned gardeners like Beatrix Potter's Mr MacGregor kept alive the traditions of their forebears behind the high walls of the kitchen garden, untroubled by their 'improving' master's plans for new lakes and copses, serpentine walks and artificial ruins. Like the old cottage gardens seen in estate villages, with flowers and vegetables, annuals and evergreens run riot, their work once again came to be admired by the Arts and Crafts designers of the nineteenth century, and many kitchen-garden features, enlarged in scale, came to occupy more prominent positions in the layout round the house. Gertrude Jekyll's herbaceous borders, paving strewn with rock plants and herbs, and use of simple trelliswork, looks back to this type of 'vernacular' gardening, with its emphasis on profusion rather than strict control and its formal framework softened by what she called the 'rough and tumble of nature'.

While herbs were a particularly important part of her palette, it was left to another lady-gardener, the American Eleanour Sinclair Rohde, to restore the herb garden to its sixteenth-century pre-eminence in the years between the wars, with innumerable articles and books on the subject. Historical re-creations like that at Hardwick, based as far as possible on contemporary documents, have helped to popularize the form, and the return of the formal *potager*, with vegetables marshalled in the mock-grandeur of a miniature parterre, and ornamental cabbages used to edge the croquet lawn, suggest that 'Humorists in Gardening' like Addison are once more on the increase.

Two formal herb gardens: (above) the parterre at Westbury Court in Gloucestershire, with box-edged beds in the seventeenth-century Dutch style – like Maynard Colchester's tall summerhouse seen beyond, built in 1702-03; (below) an outdoor garden 'room' at Cranborne in Dorset, devoted to herbs, and using the colour, shape and texture of the foliage to enhance the intricate patterns of the four plots. (Right) A blaze of colour in the kitchen garden at Floors in Roxburghshire. The walled enclosure, some way away from the house, was a particularly popular feature in Scotland, with wide herbaceous or cutting borders concealing the more utilitarian rows of fruit and vegetables on either side.

*A*pple-blossom time, (above) at Cranborne Manor, Dorset, and (below) at Penshurst Place in Kent, where the 'excellent fruit' was praised by John Evelyn as early as 1652. Orchards often occupied large sections of the kitchen garden, with wild flowers encouraged to grow in the long grass below the trees – only scythed once a year. (Left) A walk of cherry trees, underplanted with spring bulbs, leading down to the river Avon at Corsham Court in Wiltshire.

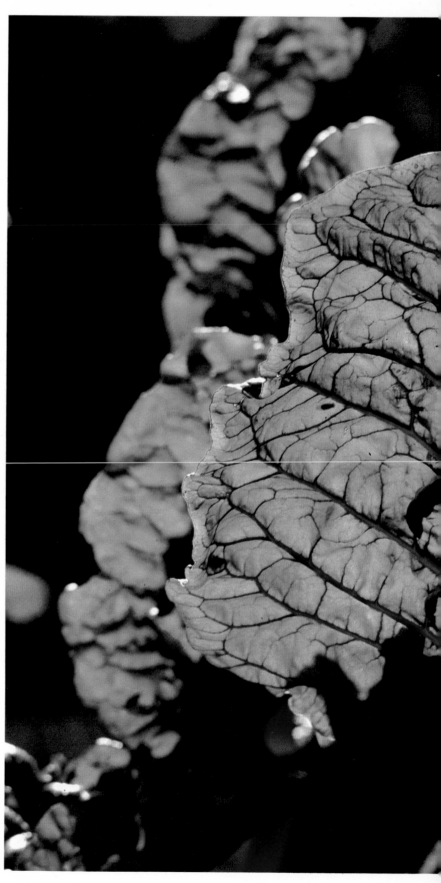

*T*he decorative value of common or garden vegetables
was realised in the seventeenth century, when formal potagers were laid out
under the influence of Louis XIV's gardener, Jean de la Quintinie.
A recent revival of the idea, with peas and beans, lettuces and cabbages,
marshalled in the mock-grandeur of a miniature parterre,
can be seen at Barnsley in Gloucestershire (above) and Tintinhull in
Somerset (below and right).

IX

CANALS, CASCADES AND FOUNTAINS

Since the walled oases of the ancient Arab world, water has been an essential adjunct of the garden, though its use grew out of purely practical needs. The narrow rill which is characteristic of the Moorish courtyard developed from irrigation channels; the fountain basin running with fresh water enabled camels and horses as well as humans to satisfy their needs more easily; while the pond or tank, stocked with fish, was an important source of food throughout the year, particularly employed by the monastic orders in northern Europe. The idea of the decorative canal, too, can be traced back to the defensive double moats of the Middle Ages, with the 'lists', where tournaments and jousts were held, lined with trees in between the two. This last development

*(Above) The Water Garden at Blenheim, with Capability Brown's lake below.
(Left) The canal at Wrest Park, Bedfordshire.*

came about in France only under the Valois, although the use of water for its purely pleasurable associations was already a feature of gardens in the ancient world. In Pliny's Tuscan Villa, the cold bath doubled up as a feature adorning the main terrace overlooked by the triclinium, so that from their couches the diners could see the water falling into the marble and hear the noise of the cascade.

Directly influenced by descriptions of such pleasure grounds, and by the excavation of Roman ruins including the Baths of Augustus and Caracalla, the architects of the Italian Renaissance revived the idea that gardens and buildings should be inter-penetrating spaces, with water as one of the main bonds between the two: the grotto and the nymphaeum, the fountain and the cascade, each in turn expressed the taming of one of nature's elemental forces by the hand of man. Elaborate waterworks and automata appealed to the scientifically inclined, and it was these which especially intrigued English visitors to Italy. Sir Henry Wotton, ambassador to Venice in 1604-12 and again in 1621-24, was delighted by a statue at Pratolino 'done by the famous hand of *Michael Angelo de Buonaroti*, in the figure of a sturdie *Woman*, *washing* and *winding* of linnen clothes; in which Acte, shee *wrings* out the water that made the *Fountaine*; which was a gracefull and naturall conceit in the Artificer'. At the same time he could appreciate the more abstract use of water as a decorative feature, for instance in a walk flanked by aqueducts, with little jets of water forming arches over it '. . . so as the *Beholder* . . . did walke as it were, under a continuall *bowre* or *Hemisphere* of water, without any drop falling on him'.

Another ambassador to Italy, Lord Lumley, who had gone as Elizabeth I's envoy to the Medici, erected fountains in her honour at Nonsuch, associating her with Diana ('Queen and huntress, chaste and fair', in Ben Jonson's words) and using water to suggest her purity. In one, a caryatid figure was seen through a veil of water; in another water gushed from the naked goddess' nipples; while a third consisted of a whole tableau in which Diana and her attendant nymphs, discovered bathing, sprayed Actaeon with water, causing antlers to grow on his head – with the result that he was devoured by his own hounds.

The prevalence of water in classical myth gave an opportunity to interpret such appropriate themes with a realism that could match any amount of carved wood, plasterwork, or tapestry inside the house. Here Ovid's *Metamorphoses* could come into their own at the turn of a stopcock, and the movement of fountains and cascades could provide the dramatic action in gardens that were increasingly seen in terms of stage sets and 'backdrops'. John Evelyn visiting Pratolino twenty-five years after Wotton found a 'Pan feeding his stock, the Water making a melodius sound through his pipe, & an Hercules whose Club yields a Showre of Water' – not to mention a grotto representing 'Vulcan & his family . . . with the huntings of Severall beasts, moving by the force of Water'.

The most famous of all such waterworks were at the Villa d'Este at Tivoli and the Villa Aldobrandini at Frascati, seen by almost every foreign visitor to Rome and imitated by innumerable English and French gardens of the late seventeenth century. Evelyn's description of Frascati seems to foreshadow the later doctrines of the 'Beautiful and the Sublime' (and the dawn of romanticism) with its account of 'a horrid Cascade seeming rather a greate River than a streame, precipitating into a large Theater of Water representing an exact & perfect Raine-bow when the sun shines out'. For the time being, however, it was the more artificial elements of the grotto with its 'hydraulic Organs & all sorts of singing birds moving, & chirping by force of the water, with severall other pageants and surprizing inventions', that were more popular with contemporaries.

Celia Fiennes describes the gilded lead fountain in the shape of a tree at Chatsworth, reconstructed in the nineteenth century but still able to give unwary visitors a soaking, and a clock in the garden at nearby Bretby 'which chimes the quarters, and when they please play Lilibolaro on the Chymes'. One of the earliest and most famous of such mechanical delights was the grotto at Enstone in Oxfordshire, created in the 1620s by the eccentric Thomas Bushell, previously a member of Francis Bacon's household. The 'Enstone Marvels', as they were called, particularly illustrated the connection between gardening and scientific advances at this period, with hydraulic effects like the silver ball rising and falling on a single jet of water, and optical experiments like the 'canopy of rain' formed to create a rainbow – in the manner of the Villa Aldobrandini. Bushell, described by a contemporary as 'a mad gim-crack yet hereditary to these Hermeticall and Proiecticall Undertakers', was also able to produce a wide variety of sounds from his waterworks, from 'the beating of a drum' to the 'chirping of a nightingale.'

Many of these ideas were also used by Isaac de Caus for Charles I and Queen Henrietta Maria (who visited the Enstone Marvels in 1635), and for the fourth Earl of Pembroke's celebrated gardens at Wilton. Here the little river Wylye was dammed to make one of the first cascades in England: a high waterfall with a curved lip once again employing the refraction of light to cause rainbows at certain times of the day. In hillier parts of the country, the French idea of a staircase of water was later adopted. That at Chatsworth was actually created by a Frenchman named Grillet in the 1690s, and, like the architecture of the house itself, was inspired by Louis XIV's Marly. A temple or cascade house, designed by Thomas Archer, was built at its head in 1711, with a fountain gushing from its cupola and spreading a film of water over the three tiers of the dome. From here, 'out of the mouths of beasts, pipes, urns, etc' in Defoe's words, 'a whole river descends the slope of a hill a quarter of a mile in length, over steps, with a terrible noise, and broken appearance'.

The cascade at Dyrham in Gloucestershire must have been equally dramatic, for Stephen Switzer records that 'the Weight of the Water, and the Falls are so great, that the Noise very near equals the Billows of a raging Sea, and may be heard at a very great Distance'. However, all that remains is the stone figure of Neptune at the top, striking the rock in vain with his 'exalted Trident'. The relationship between the internal architecture of the Baroque house and the 'outdoor rooms' of its surrounding gardens has already been suggested, and water was one of the chief means by which this was achieved. As well as the 'staircase' of water, there were the so-called *buffets d'eau* or tiered arrangements of fountains, imitating the sideboard of the state dining room with its brimming silver ewers, cisterns and wine-coolers. Above all, there was the long canal, equivalent to the enfilade or axial vista that was the hallmark of the Baroque interior.

While the interest in elaborate waterworks came from Italy by way of France, the idea of the canal and the technical development of dams, sluices and aqueducts used to bring water to the most unpromising terrain, came primarily from the Low Countries. William Blathwayt's hundred-yard-long canal at Dyrham, containing trout, perch and carp, as well as two tame swans, must have been influenced by his frequent visits to Holland as William III's Secretary-at-War. The Boeveys' canal at nearby Flaxley Abbey has been connected with their marriage into an Amsterdam merchant family, while another neighbour, Maynard Colchester of Westbury Court, had trading interests in Bristol which may explain the overwhelmingly Dutch character of his garden, with its three canals lined by yew hedges, restored by the National Trust in the 1970s. Whereas the canal was almost invariably placed on axis with the house in France, emphasizing the limitless vistas of Le Nôtre, those at Dyrham and Westbury were terminated by subsidiary buildings: in the first case an orangery, and in the second a tall gazebo like those seen in the paintings of Pieter de Hooch or Cornelis Troost – the ancestor of eighteenth-century fishing temples like that at Stoke-by-Nayland in Suffolk.

In the short-lived Baroque style that flourished under William and Mary and Queen Anne, the axial canal was occasionally favoured, as at Wrest Park in Bedfordshire (with Archer's domed temple at the end), at Easton Neston, or even at a comparatively small squire's house like Erddig in North Wales. By 1712, however, John James' translation of d'Argenville's *Theory and Practice of Gardening* was already proposing a canal on the cross-axis, some way from the house, large enough for a small flotilla of boats, and serving 'for an Inclosure to separate the Park and Garden'. The sides of these canals, like Charles Bridgeman's, may still have been straight-edged, with circular or octagonal basins at the ends (or in the centre) to give them variety, but it was only a matter of time before Hogarth's serpentine 'line of beauty' softened their contours and gave them the appearance of natural lakes. As with so many other advances towards the 'Picturesque', the catalyst was William Kent. In Horace Walpole's words, '. . . of all the beauties he added to the face of this beautiful country, none surpassed his management of water. Adieu to canals, circular basons, and cascades tumbling down marble steps, that last absurd magnificence of Italian and French villas . . . the gentle stream was taught to serpentize seemingly at its pleasure, and where discontinued by different levels, its course appeared to be concealed by thickets properly interspersed, and glittered again at a distance where it might be supposed naturally to arrive.'

If the canal was superseded by the lake, in imitation of Claude's ethereal visions, the cascade (in the old artificial meaning of the word) was replaced by the waterfall, in the manner of Ruysdael and Hobbema. Stephen Switzer had already praised the cascade at Dyrham for running 'not over polish'd Masonry, but over the roughest Frostwork and rugged Stone', while theorists like Roger de Piles, writing on landscape painting, had pointed to the future in their praise of rocks, '. . . of themselves gloomy, and only proper for solitudes; but . . . when they have waters, either proceeding from or washing them, they give an infinite pleasure, and seem to have a soul which animates them, and makes them sociable'. Almost Chinese in their attribution of human values to inanimate Nature, de Piles' theories reinforced the search for 'Sharawadgi' as Sir William Temple had called it, the idealization of nature within the microcosm of a man-made landscape. Kent's cascades in 'Venus' Vale' at Rousham, with their broad arches of rusticated rockwork, lead swans, and stone urns, may not seem 'natural' today, but in their sylvan setting they look forward to the more rugged waterfalls created by Capability Brown at Blenheim, and Charles Hamilton at Bowood.

Fountains too were to be condemned in the reaction against man-made contrivances. John Shebbeare's *Letters on the English Nation* written in 1755 in the guise of a mythical Italian visitor, 'Battista Angeloni', report that 'the *jet d'eau* is quite out of fashion in this kingdom . . . in truth, it is always unnatural to see water rising into the air, contrary to its original tendency.' But whereas the long canal and the stepped cascade were never to make a significant comeback in England, the fountain returned in the nineteenth century with the fashion for Italianate gardens, laid out along architectural lines. A favourite form was the triple-tiered *compotière*, found repeatedly in Victorian silver and ceramics, and ultimately deriving from the antique candelabrum rediscovered by Raphael and his contemporaries. But the single jet of majestic proportions, like Paxton's great 'Emperor Fountain' at Chatsworth, also told of new engineering skills brought by the Industrial Revolution.

The introduction of exotic water-loving plants – in which Paxton himself took a special interest – also created a demand for lily ponds. Bog gardens, like that at Sezincote, made by damming a small stream to make a chain of ponds, were equally popular, sometimes imitating the miniature river valleys of Japanese gardens. Towards the end of the nineteenth century, the publication of illustrated books on garden history also encouraged a return to the artificial water garden: Achille Duchêne's west parterre at Blenheim recalled the romance of Eugène Atget's photographs of Versailles; while Harold Peto's narrow rills, cut through the woods between the house and lake at Buscot, transposed the cooling channels of the sun-baked Alhambra to the damp and leafy landscape of rural Oxfordshire.

Water is still one of the essential elements of the country-house garden, and, like the use of glass in modern buildings, has come to be valued above all for its reflective powers. The round pond at Knightshayes, surrounded by a dark green wall of clipped yew planted in the 1930s, looks back to the mirror surfaces of the early-eighteenth-century Moon Ponds at Studley Royal, seen from the thickly-wooded hills above. Ben Nicholson's white marble 'wall' seen doubled in a still, black square of water in Sir Geoffrey Jellicoe's garden at Sutton Place, created in the 1980s, belongs to the same tradition: a return to the simple elements of the landscape garden – trees and grass, water and sky – unifying the works of man and nature in an ideal whole.

The Atlas Fountain at Castle Howard, acquired by the 7th Earl of Carlisle at the Great Exhibition in 1851, and installed in the centre of the south parterre by W.A. Nesfield.

Classical reflections: (above) the Doric Temple at Barnsley in Gloucestershire, and (right) the Pin Mill at Bodnant in North Wales. The latter, built about 1740 as a summerhouse at Woodchester, in Gloucestershire, was acquired by the 2nd Lord Aberconway and moved to its present site in 1938. It was he who also made the canal, on one of the five Italianate terraces below the house, with spectacular views over the Conway valley to the peak of Snowdon.

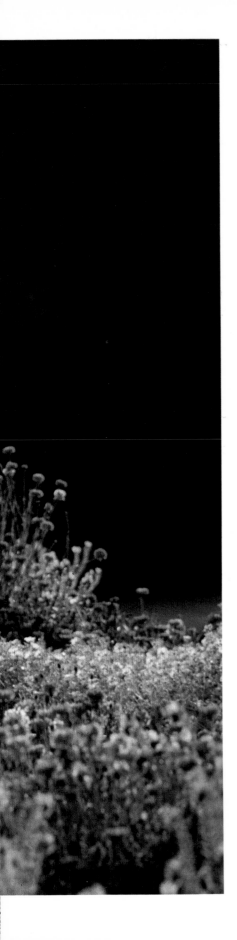

CANALS, CASCADES AND FOUNTAINS

*Water, sunlight and shadow: (above) a 'tazza' fountain on the terraces at Bowood in Wiltshire,
(below) a winged monster from the cascade at Bramham Park in Yorkshire, and (left) a copy of Verrocchio's
Boy with a Dolphin at Crathes Castle. Italian Renaissance gardens, seen by the English 'milords'
on the Grand Tour, encouraged an interest in elaborate waterworks which survived the 'Natural Landscape'
school, and came back into fashion in the early nineteenth century.*

137

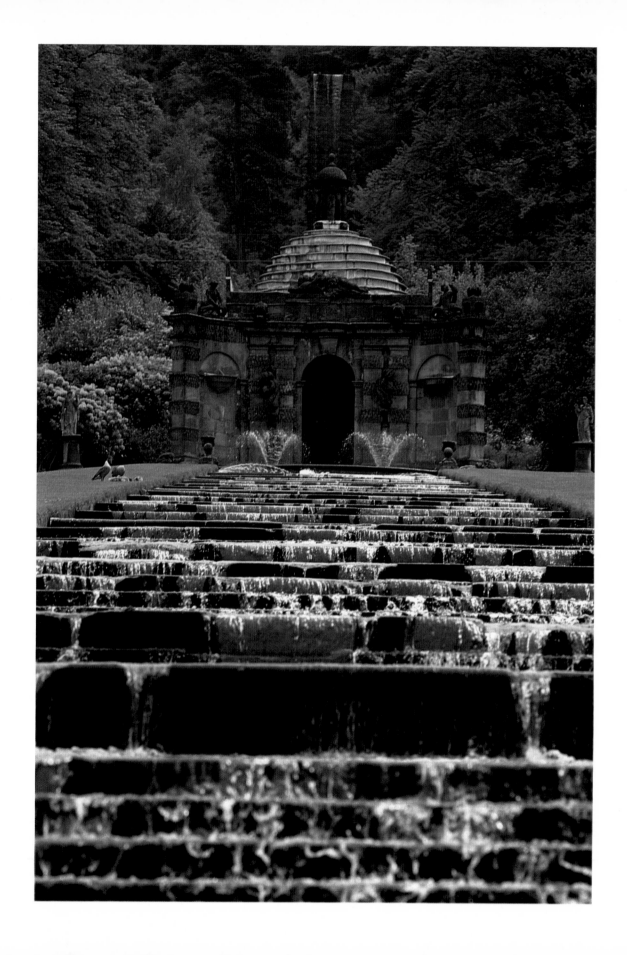

Staircases of water: (above) the cascade at West Wycombe, probably designed by a Frenchman named Jolivet in the 1740s; (below) the grottoes at Studley Royal; and (left) the cascade at Chatsworth, with Thomas Archer's temple, built in 1711, at its head.

'Picturesque' gardeners were to reject such man-made contrivances in favour of natural waterfalls, in the manner of Jacob Ruysdael and Salvator Rosa: (overleaf) Charles Hamilton's cascade at Bowood, constructed in 1785-87 and (right) Capability Brown's at Blenheim, designed in the 1760s.

X

LAKES AND
BRIDGES

But when the Lake shall these sweet Grounds adorn,
And bright expanding like the eye of Morn,
Reflect whate'er above its surface rise,
The Hills, the Rocks, the Woods, and varying Skies,
Then will the wild and beautiful combine,
And Taste and Beauty grace your whole Design.

Thus Lord Irwin was urged to improve his landscape at Temple Newsam by the anonymous author of *The Rise and Progress of the Present Taste in Planting Parks, Pleasure Grounds, Gardens, Etc.*, published in 1767. The eighteenth-century passion for lakes, sweeping away the narrow geometry of the long canal, was central to the idea of picturesque gardening. But the technical knowl-

(Left) The Palladian Bridge at Stourhead in Wiltshire, built by Henry Hoare between 1760 and 1765. (Above) Swans on the lake at Osterley, Middlesex.

edge that made it possible, the study of hydraulics, central to dam-building and the management of water-flow, was pioneered by the monks – particularly the Benedictines and Cistercians – of the Middle Ages. Their chains of stew-ponds stocked with fish, to be eaten on Fridays and other fast-days, as well as in Lent, are indeed the origin of several country-house lakes – like those at Nostell Priory and Woburn Abbey.

One of the first instances of a lake being excavated for purely pleasurable purposes in an English park (instead of being a fish tank or an adaptation of a defensive moat) was made in connection with the famous Elvetham entertainment given by Lord Hertford for Queen Elizabeth I in September 1591. Like so many other features of the Elizabethan garden this lake had an emblematic function, for it was laid out in the shape of a vast crescent moon, representing the Queen as the moon goddess, Cynthia, Diana or Belphoebe. Only three years after the defeat of the Spanish Armada, it particularly symbolized her role as mistress of the seas, for within it were three islands: one with trees cut like the masts of ships; another with a fort built by Neptune in defence of England; and a third with a mount twenty feet high, planted in ascending circles of privet, representing Spain – 'you ugly monster creeping from the South to spoyle these blessed fields of Albion'. In the firework display at the end of the evening, the monster was overcome by gunfire from Neptune's mount, anticipating the mock naval battles held on many lakes in the eighteenth century.

Roy Strong has traced the origin of such water festivals back to Charles IX's Fontainebleau and the entertainments held at Bayonne in connection with the treaty between France and Spain of 1565. Francis Bacon, who served in the English embassy in Paris in the following decade, may also have been inspired by French precedents in creating his ponds at Gorhambury, over four acres in extent. According to Aubrey, these were lined with coloured pebbles, while one of them had 'a curious banquetting-house of Roman architecture' on an island in the centre. Robert Cecil, Bacon's close friend, created a naturalistic river, crossed by several wooden bridges, immediately outside the garden at Theobalds, almost certainly inspired by Pliny's description of his layout at Tusculum – where the formal elements near the villa were deliberately contrasted with the informal beyond. But this has to be seen as a rare and isolated precursor of the eighteenth-century serpentine lake, planned to look like a majestic river winding through the landscape, rather than a static pond or reservoir.

In the Baroque period, large ponds were often created either to terminate canals or as independent features, though almost always of regular geometrical shape. As Batty Langley put it as late as 1728, 'the Circle, Elipsis, Octagon, and mix'd Figures composed of Geometrical Squares, Parallelograms, and Arches of Circles, make very beautiful Figures for Water . . . but of them all, the Circle is the most grand and beautiful'. The only irregular sheets of water were likely to be the reservoirs that fed the fountains, cascades and other waterworks, often placed at the furthest edge of the garden, and at the highest point. That at Dyrham, according to Switzer, took up 'near an Acre of Ground, and at the head is eighteen or twenty Foot deep; it has an Island in the Middle planted with Trees, contains Variety of the finest Water-Fowl, is well stock'd with most Sorts of Fish; and here you may sail in a Ship on a Mountain . . .'.

Elaborate duck decoys, like those shown in Kip's engraving of Haughton in Nottinghamshire, were often arranged on larger ponds of this kind, reflecting the same interest in natural history seen in Bogdany's contemporary paintings of wildfowl, and the popularity of aviaries as garden features. Visiting the lake at Wimborne St Giles in 1754, Bishop Pococke was shown 'a sea duck which lays in rabbits burrows, from which they are call'd Burrow ducks, & are something like the shell drake'. At Well Vale in Lincolnshire, the Muscovies that bred in profusion on the lakes above and below the house were so highly prized by their owner, Mr Bateman, that he adopted them for his family coat-of-arms in place of more conventional heraldic birds.

The shapes of lakes created in the picturesque landscape garden were largely dictated by the lie of the land, making use of valleys that already existed – even if vast teams of 'jocund labourers' were needed to make their outlines less regular, contributing an island here and a promontory there. Consequently, very few actually set out to copy an admired Old Master painting. The view over the lake to the pantheon at Stourhead is said to have been based on Claude's *Coast View of Delos with Aeneas* (now in the National Gallery in London); and at Castle Howard, Vanbrugh's lake and bridge, combined with a square building (the Temple of the Winds) and a round one (the Mausoleum), may have deliberately invoked the ingredients of other celebrated Claudes, like the *Pastoral Landscape with the Ponte Molle* (now in the Birmingham City Art Gallery). But on the whole it was the detailed treatment of smaller areas which were more likely to imitate the painter's brush, like parts of the lakeside at Painshill known to have been based on sketches by Salvator Rosa.

Sir William Chambers' account of Chinese gardening, published in 1757, stressed the infinite variety possible in the treatment of lakes and rivers – from the planting of reeds and weeping willows to the introduction of artificial rocks 'worn into irregular forms by the action of the waves . . . which they join with a bluish cement', and 'trunks of decayed trees, sometimes erect, and at other times lying on the ground, being very nice about their forms, and the colour of the bark and moss on them.' Above all, Chambers admired the way 'the termination of their lakes they always hide, leaving room for the imagination to work' – a cardinal rule of the later Picturesque landscape. As William Gilpin put it, in the 1790s, criticizing Capability Brown for failing 'more in river-making than in any of his attempts', '. . . an artificial lake has sometimes a good effect; but neither propriety, nor beauty can arise from it, unless the heads and extremities of it are perfectly well managed and concealed . . . you must always suppose it a portion of a larger piece of water'.

The bridge played an important part in such deceptions. Brown himself often used them to conceal dams, as at Wotton, where it came as a surprise to visitors to find the river at a higher level on one side than on the other; while at Kenwood the dummy bridge at the end of the lake is still no more than a wooden silhouette. At Kedleston, Robert Adam's three-arched bridge is combined with a spectacular cascade, an idea probably taken from the Falls of Terni which he had sketched during his time in Rome. Henry Wise's much earlier artificial river at Blenheim, one of the first in Britain, also fell in a cascade below Vanbrugh's monumental bridge. But later admirers of the Picturesque found their difference in scale absurd, and it was for this reason that Capability Brown was called in to flood the whole valley of the little stream known as the Glyme in 1764. The result, drowning not only the cascade, but many of the rooms which Vanbrugh had contrived within the piers of the bridge, was so spectacular that one can believe Brown's reputed boast on seeing the work completed: 'Thames, Thames, you will never forgive me'.

What contemporaries most criticized about Capability Brown's lakes was the comparative nakedness of their shores, perhaps implicit in Dr Johnson's remark to James Boswell when they visited Blenheim in 1776: 'You and I, Sir! have, I think, seen together the extremes of what can be seen in Britain: the wild rough island of Mull, and Blenheim Park.' But it is true that Brown was often dealing with flat countryside where the maximum of water needed to be seen from the house – unlike the Welsh border country, to which Payne Knight and Uvedale Price were accustomed, where raised viewpoints were normal, enabling lakes and rivers to be seen above riparian vegetation. William Shenstone, whose garden at the Leasowes also benefited from a hilly terrain, stipulated that 'the eye should always look rather down upon water', and Richard Wilson's early paintings of Wilton show spectators high on the hillside gazing down on placid waters, as if on the unplumbed depths of Lake Nemi.

Reflections, whether of trees, bridges or other buildings, were carefully calculated. Milton wrote of the 'Lake, that to the fringed Bank with Myrtle crownd, Her chrystall mirror holds', and such Virgilian imagery was brought to life in gardens like Stourhead, where Joseph Spence particularly admired the placing of the Temple of Apollo – so that, 'when you sit deep within the Temple, you wou'd think it was built close by the Lake, & when you walk round the Latter below, you are almost continually entertaind by the Reflection of it, in the water.'

Bridges were particularly designed with their reflection in mind: a high arch forming almost a perfect circle seen in the still waters. The Palladian bridges at Wilton, Stowe and Prior Park, based on one of the architect's unexecuted schemes for the Rialto in Venice, are among the most successful of all English garden buildings, not only because they suggest a far more substantial barrier of water than actually exists, but because they also act as 'eyecatchers' from a distance, and give an architectural framework for the views to be enjoyed from their high colonnades.

Gothick and Chinese bridges employed the same architectural language as the temples and pavilions which dotted the mid-eighteenth-century park, but Richard Payne Knight poured scorn on such fantasies in his 'didactic poem', *The Landscape* (1794):

> The stately arch, high-rais'd with massive stone;
> The pond'rus flag, that forms a bridge alone;
> The prostrate tree, or rudely propt-up beam,
> That leads the path across the foaming stream;
> May each the scene with diff'rent beauty grace,
> If shewn with judgement in its proper place.
> But false refinement vainly strives to please,
> With the thin, fragile bridge of the Chinese;
> Light and fantastical, yet stiff and prim,
> The child of barren fancy turn'd to whim . . .

Other buildings considered suitable for the lake included fishing temples, like Robert Adam's at Kedleston, so contrived that you could put a rod straight out of the Venetian window of his charming neo-classical banqueting room, and complete with cold bath and boat houses below. Forts and bastions were another favourite feature, for barges and sailing ships of a considerable size were often kept on the lake, and complete naval actions could be enacted for the benefit of a country-house owner and his guests. At West Wycombe, after the dedication of the West Portico in 1771, the company dressed in bacchanalian 'skins wreathed with vine leaves' repaired to the lake for further 'Paeans and libations' and 'discharges of cannon' from several boats – while on another occasion the fun was nearly marred by the captain of one of the yachts being struck by a large piece of wadding from the cannon of an opponent. At Newstead Abbey, the fifth Lord Byron, formerly a Captain in the Royal Navy, had much more professional battles with the gamekeepers press-ganged into being sailors for the day, while Fort Henry at Exton – perhaps the most elaborate of such buildings to survive – was built by another seafaring family, the Noels.

The grotto was another obvious accompaniment to the lake, often built at the head of the valley so that the waters could appear to gush from its dark recesses – even if the majority actually came from hidden land drains. One of the most famous was that at Stourhead, and Sir Richard Colt Hoare's description of his gardens there includes an account of how 'the native stone, forming natural stalactites, and the "fresh water and seats in the living rock" [Virgil, *Aeneid*, 1.164-6] compose the interior of this cavern; the *sombre* appearance of which is relieved by two figures very appropriately placed' – the languorous 'Nymph of the Grot', and the River God from whose urn the source of the Stour bursts and flows through the cave. Grottoes were usually intended to evoke a mood of awesome melancholy, conjured up by Sir Samuel Garth in his poem on Claremont of 1715:

> A grot there was with hoary moss o'ergrown,
> Rough with rude shells, and arch'd with mould'ring stone;
> Sad silence reigns within the lonesome wall,
> And weeping rills but whisper as they fall;
> The clasping ivies up the ruin creep,
> And there the bat and drowsy beetle sleep.

On the other hand, Thomas Wright's grotto at Hampton Court House, built by Lord Halifax for his mistress, a famous opera singer, was on the edge of a heart-shaped lake, and encrusted with shells and minerals under a dome representing the starry heavens. The two alcoves representing dawn and dusk probably contained beds, warmed by two miniature fireplaces, and these must instantly have dispelled any feelings of gloom. Although there were specialists in the making of grottoes, like 'Mr Castles of

Marybone', author of the famous one at Wimborne St Giles, or Joseph and Josiah Lane, creators of the still more spectacular grotto on the lake at Painshill, the arrangement of stones and shells was often carried out by gifted amateurs like the Duchess of Richmond and her daughters at Goodwood, or Mrs Delany and her friend the Duchess of Portland at Bulstrode.

So prevalent was the fashion for lakes in the eighteenth century that almost every country house, large or small, could boast one by the early nineteenth. The Victorian and Edwardian contribution to their appearance was largely confined to planting, and with a particular emphasis on exotic trees and shrubs, notable for their autumn colour. Thus the string of lakes at Sheffield Park in Sussex, some created by Brown and some by Repton, were extended in the 1880s when the rockery-builder James Pulham also constructed a cascade and water garden. The red and gold foliage of trees brought from the Himalayas or the Americas, reflected in the water, and backed by older plantations of hardwoods, make it in many ways a culmination of Picturesque gardening.

The Lake at Hever Castle, seen from Frank Pearson's Italianate loggia. Constructed in the early years of this century by William Waldorf Astor, but still very much in the 'Picturesque' tradition.

*S*wans and Canada geese with their young at Sudbury in Derbyshire, and (right) a black swan on
the lake at Claremont in Surrey. The grass amphitheatre, recently restored by the National Trust, was created
by Charles Bridgeman for the 1st Duke of Newcastle in the early 1720s. It originally overlooked
a round pond, which William Kent enlarged and 'naturalised' to form the present lake before 1738.

*E*arly summer colour on the lake at Stourhead, with the Temple of Flora, built in 1744-46 and one of the earliest of Henry Hoare's garden buildings, on the right. Virgil's <u>Aeneid</u> provided the inspiration for many features of the garden, and the lake itself recalls Aeneas' vision of Father Tiber, while sleeping on the river bank, and his oath on waking: 'whatever spring may fill the pools which are your home, and wherever you yourself emerge in grandeur from the soil, always shall you be celebrated by me . . .'. The Temple itself bears the inscription 'Procul, o procul este profani' ('Begone, you who are uninitiated! Begone!'), the words spoken by the Cumaean Sybil before leading Aeneas into the underworld.

The Nymph of the Grotto at Stourhead, evoking the cave in the haven near Carthage where Aeneas and his men took refuge from a storm. The grotto not only offered a view of the lake framed in the cave-mouth, but also contained a cold plunge. As Henry Hoare wrote in the hot summer of 1764, 'a souse in that delicious bath and grot, filld with fresh magic, is Asiatick luxury.'

(Right) The Palladian Bridge at Stowe, built before 1745, a combination of belvedere and eyecatcher, whose monumental proportions seem to enlarge the narrow stretch of water that it crosses.

*T*he bridge as garden ornament: (left) Vanbrugh's monumental arch at Blenheim – its lower
rooms flooded when Capability Brown raised the level of the water; (above) Robert Adam's bridge at
Kedleston, placed over the cascade between two lakes; and (below) the sweeping curves
of Sir John Soane's bridge over the Ouse at Tyringham.

*A culmination of picturesque gardening: Sheffield Park in East Sussex. (Left) The falls
made by Pulham and Sons for the 3rd Earl of Sheffield in 1883; (above) the stone bridge between the
First and Second Lakes. The gardens were originally laid out by Capability Brown in the 1770s,
but with a wide variety of trees planted in the early years of this century, and
particularly chosen for their autumn colour.*

XI

WILD GARDENS AND SHRUBBERIES

The idea of the wild garden or 'wilderness' developed from the sacred grove of trees, one of the oldest of all garden features since it dates back to the time of primitive man in the forest. Tree cults arose from the comparison of human life with the growth and death of trees – which the ancient Egyptians considered 'eternal souls'. The Greeks also believed in the mystical nature of the sacred grove, but at the same time gave it an intellectual basis: Plato's Academy was thus held in a plantation of olive trees, not only because they provided shade, but because their regular planting patterns were conducive to thought and contemplation. Teaching in the later Lyceum of Aristotle was actually peripatetic, conducted while walking along the tree-lined paths of the grove,

(Left) A woodland glade at Exbury in Hampshire. (Above) Bluebells in the long grass at Hever Castle, Kent.

161

and this concept of the wilderness as a place for intellectual pursuits was carried over into the gardens of seventeenth- and eighteenth-century England. Danckerts' picture of the Duke and Duchess of Lauderdale promenading in the Wilderness at Ham shows them accompanied by their chaplain with a book of sermons; Stephen Switzer records that the wilderness at Dyrham was 'a place for the sublimest Studies . . . and here are small Desks erected in Seats for that purpose'; while Bishop Pococke, who admired the woodland walks at Wimborne St Giles in the 1750s, noticed that 'in all the houses & seats are books in hanging Glass cases'.

Just as the Romans dedicated their groves to particular deities, so the *bosco* of the Italian Renaissance gave opportunities to interpret scenes from classical mythology. The story of Diana and Actaeon from Ovid's *Metamorphoses*, was a perennial favourite for its combination of woods and water, humans and animals, and the Grove of Diana at Nonsuch created by Lord Lumley as a tribute to Elizabeth I, may well have been based on gardens seen during his embassy to Florence in the 1560s. A German visitor, Paul Hentzner, described it in 1598 as 'a valley, thick set with pitch-trees and the sharp-pointed Cypress; by name Gargaphie, sacred to the active Diana'. The dark shades of this grove, beyond the formal parterres of the main garden, were intended to impart a feeling of pleasing melancholy – an attribute that was once again connected in the Elizabethan mind with imaginative and intellectual powers.

In the Middle Ages, the cold and dry qualitites of the melancholy humour were considered inimical to life, but Renaissance thinkers such as the Florentine humanist Marsilio Ficino resurrected the Aristotelian idea that such a temperament was a mark of genius. The title page of Burton's *Anatomy of Melancholy* (1612) shows the philosopher Democritus of Abdera seeking the shade of the greenwood tree, outside the bounds of a formal garden, while the same image can be found in Isaac Oliver's portraits of young gallants like Lord Herbert of Cherbury, brooding alone in naturalistic woodland settings. In Burton's words, 'what is more pleasant than to walk alone in some solitary grove betwixt Wood and Water, by a Brook side, to meditate upon some delightsome and plesant subject . . .'.

Francis Bacon visualized his ideal garden only four years later as having a '*Heath* or *Desart*' beyond the main parterres, which he wished 'to be framed as much as may be, to a *Natural Wildness*'. More in the nature of a shrubbery than a grove, it was to have '*Thickets*, made onely of *Sweet-Briar*, and honny-suckle, and some Wilde Vine amongst; And the Ground set with *Violets*, *Strawberries*, and *Prime-Roses* . . . here and there, not in any Order. I like also little *Heaps*, in the nature of *Mole-hils*, (such as are in *Wilde Heaths*) to be set, some with Wild Thyme; some with Pincks; some with Germander . . .' To modern ears, deserts and wildernesses imply barren wastes untouched by the hand of man, let alone the 'improving' gardener, but in the seventeenth century such terms were used for highly artificial *bosquets*, like those created by Le Nôtre at Versailles – merely because trees or shrubs were allowed to grow here without being trained into topiary shapes, and because there was an element of mystery or surprise in not being able to see the full layout of paths and compartments from any one point.

The 'Grove or Wilderness', which Timothy Nourse recommended as the third and last section of the pleasure garden in his *Campania Foelix* (1700) was 'wholly to be design'd for Boscage' and was to contain 'up and down Little private Alleys or Walks of Beech . . . Tufts of Cypress-Trees, planted in the Form of a Theater . . . likewise Fir-Trees in some negligent Order, as also Lawrels, Philyrea's, Bays, Tumarist, the Silac Tree, *Althea* Fruits, Pyracanthe,' and a host of other evergreens, so that it should 'represent a perpetual Spring'. 'In a word,' he concludes, 'let this Third Region or Wilderness be Natural-Artificial; that is, let all things be dispos'd with that cunning, as to deceive us into a belief of a real Wilderness or Thicket, and yet to be furnished with all the Varieties of Nature.' If the basic ideals of the Picturesque landscape garden are already inherent in this passage, it took the doctrines of philosophers like Locke and Shaftesbury to identify the 'natural liberties' of the English constitution with a style of gardening which would reflect that freedom: to pose the unfettered wilderness against the absolutist parterre.

In Shaftesbury's *The Moralists*, published in 1709, Theocles, the spokesman of enthusiasm, looks for a supreme creator to the heart of the natural world, and here – 'The Wildness pleases. We seem to live alone with Nature. We view her in her inmost Recesses, and Contemplate her with more Delight in these original Wilds, than in the artificial Labyrinths and feign'd Wildernesses of the Palace . . .' Taken to its extremes, such thinking could have denied the validity of gardening altogether, and Kent's attempt to plant dead trees in Kensington Gardens (greeted with derision even by his most loyal supporters) showed that there was a point at which the imitation of nature could lapse into absurdity. But it was the serpentine paths of the wilderness – at first a deliberate contrast with the axial vistas of the main parterre – that were developed into the circuit walk of the typical eighteenth-century landscape park, and it is this development which gives it such importance in the history of English taste.

Another early characteristic that was to affect the future of the wild garden was the predominance of evergreens in its planting. Writing in the *Spectator* in September 1712, Joseph Addison advocated the idea of a '*Winter Garden*, which should consist of such Trees only as never cast their leaves'. Having himself devoted 'a whole Acre of Ground for the executing of it', he goes on to describe the walls 'covered with Ivy instead of Vines. The Laurel, the Hornbeam, and the Holly, with many other Trees and Plants of the same Nature, grow so thick in it, that you cannot imagine a more lively scene . . . It is very pleasant, at the same Time, to see the Several Kinds of Birds retiring into this little green Spot, and enjoying themselves among the Branches and Foliage, when my great Garden . . . does not afford a single Leaf for their Shelter.'

The increasing number of flowering shrubs available from British nurserymen in the eighteenth century also helped to popularize informal planting. One of the most famous was James Gordon, who began as gardener to Lord Petre at Thorndon Hall, but who set up in business at Mile End after his employer's death in 1743. 'Before him,' wrote the naturalist Peter Collinson, 'I never knew or heard of any man that could raise the dusty seeds of kalmia's, rhododendrons, or azalea's. These charming hardy shrubs, that excel all others in his care, he furnishes to every curious garden; all the nurserymen and gardeners come to him for them.' Collinson himself helped Gordon to acquire North American plants, through the Quaker John Bartram of Pennsylvania, praised by Linnaeus as one of the greatest of field botanists – while Mark Catesby's journey to the Carolinas and the Bahamas in 1722-26, sponsored by Sir Hans Sloane and other members of the Royal Society, opened up another area of interest. Above all, it was Sir Joseph Banks, who accompanied Captain Cook on his voyage round the world in 1768-71 and brought back a vast range of Australasian plants, who enriched the palette of the garden designer in the latter part of the century.

The appearance of 'natural' growth in the wild garden was early on achieved by a profusion of climbing plants. Thus, Batty Langley proposed 'that all the Trees of your shady Walks and Groves be planted with Sweet-Brier, White Jessemine, and Honey-suckles, environ'd at Bottom with a small Circle of Dwarf-Stock, Candy-Turf, and Pinks', and Kent's evergreen screens at Rousham were enlivened with flowery under-plantings. In a letter of 1750, describing a tour of the different vantage points in fasci-nating detail, John Macclary, the gardener at Rousham, writes: 'here you think the Laurel produces a Rose, the Holly a Syringa, the Yew a Lilac and the sweet honey-suckle is peeping out from under every leafe, in short they are so mixt together, that you'd think every Leafe of the Evergreens produced one flower or another'. The *ferme ornée*, pioneered by Philip Southcote at Woburn Farm in Surrey, has been described as a form of linear wilderness planting, with trees and shrubs planted in the old hedges and a border of herbaceous plants and bulbs in front – what Joseph Spence dubbed a 'half-garden' in his 'Letter to the Rev Mr Wheeler' of 1751.

The late-eighteenth-century wilderness, by this time more likely to be called the pleasure ground, was a more colourful place than it might now seem, when only the larger trees survive. Capability Brown's at Petworth, for instance, included 'Spireas, Persian jasmins, Virginian Sheemachs, tamarisks, bird and double cherries, American maples, sea buckthorns, trumpet flowers, roses, candleberry trees, broom, sweet briars, laburnums, lilacs and acacias', all supplied by the Kensington nurseryman John Williamson. The serpentine paths included one planned to go 'through ye Laurels leading up to the Seat where the Duchess of Somerset used to drink her coffee', and 'incidents' of this kind were encouraged as long as they did not look too artificial.

Richard Payne Knight once again indicated what was allowable:

> The cover'd seat, that shelters from the storm,
> May oft a feature in the Landscape form;
> Whether compos'd of native stumps and roots,
> It spreads the creeper's rich fantastic shoots;
> Or, rais'd with stones, irregularly pil'd
> It seems some cavern, desolate and wild:
> But still of dress and ornament beware;
> And hide each formal trace of art with care:
> Let clust'ring ivy o'er its sides be spread,
> And moss and weeds grow scattered o'er its head.

Just such a cave is described by Horace Walpole at Claremont in 1763, and his account of a *fête* held there exactly captures the kind of rococo spirit in which the pleasure ground was used: '. . . from thence we passed in to the wood, and the ladies formed a circle of chairs before the mouth of a cave, which was overhung to a vast height with woodbines, lilacs and laburnums, and dignified with tall stately cypresses. On the descent of the hill were placed French horns; the abigails, servants and neighbours wandering below by the river; in short, it was Parnassus, as Watteau would have painted it.'

Caves and quarries (also recommended by Payne Knight) were the ancestors of the

Victorian rock garden, like that at Biddulph Grange, often using James Pulham's artificial boulders, manufactured to suggest the natural stratification of a sandstone outcrop. Thomas Moore's handbook on ferns, published in the late 1840s, inaugurated a passion for collecting different types that lasted until the end of the century, and outdoor rockeries or glens tended to be planted with the hardier varieties. A notable example is Bateman's collection of ferns in his glen at Biddulph. American gardens, devoted to North American trees and shrubs, were popular too, and those designed by Humphry Repton at Ashridge, Bulstrode and Woburn Abbey (among others) were planted with a freedom and irregularity thought to simulate their native habitat.

International exhibitions, beginning with that at the Crystal Palace in 1851, later stimulated an interest in the gardening traditions of other countries. Lamport Hall in Northamptonshire can boast one of the earliest collections of gnomes brought back from Switzerland, and placed in a specially constructed rock garden. On a more serious level, the opening of Japan after the Meiji restoration in 1868 led to the creation of a number of Japanese gardens, like those at Heale House in Wiltshire and Tatton Park in Cheshire, using stone lanterns, rocks and a number of rare imported trees and shrubs. Above all, travel in northern India and Nepal inspired the great woodland gardens of the twentieth century, like the Dell at Bodnant – with its rare rhododendrons and azaleas under a canopy of sheltering oaks – or the peninsula at Inverewe on the north-west coast of Scotland – thanks to the Gulf Stream, one of the best sub-tropical gardens in Europe. Treasures such as these are not the least of the legacies left by Britain's Imperial past.

(Right) Azaleas in the Dell at Bodnant, in North Wales.
The valley of the little river Hiraethlin was first
planted with shrubs in the 1930s by the 2nd Lord Aberconway,
one of the great horticulturists of his day.

*H*ardy exotics in a woodland setting at Leonardslee, near Horsham in Sussex. (Above) A rhododendron in the Loderi Garden, named after famous rhododendron hybrids first raised here by Sir Edmund Loder. (Right) the Rock Garden, with azaleas, conifers, and trachycarpus palms.

*I*nformality in the 'jardin anglais': (above) the Medicean Lion at
Kedleston strolls through banks of rhododendrons; (below) spring wild flowers
on the terrace at Farnborough, Warwickshire; and (right) autumn crocus
at Tyninghame in East Lothian.

*T*he Nuttery at Sissinghurst Castle, Kent (left), fulfilling
V. Sackville-West's ideal of 'the strictest formality of design, with
the maximum informality in planting'. (Above) Leucojum at
Sissinghurst, and buttercups at Cranborne.

173

XII

ORANGERIES AND CONSERVATORIES

A native of southern China, thought to have been introduced to the West by Marco Polo, the orange tree has been prized by English gardeners above almost any other fruit since the late sixteenth century. The orangery, the conservatory and the green-house – almost interchangeable terms throughout this period – were devised to conserve it and other tender 'greens' (such as bays, oleanders, myrtles, aloes and variegated hollies) during the harsh winter months, when they would otherwise have been killed by frost.

Elizabeth I's famous minister, William Cecil, Lord Burghley, may have been the first to grow oranges in this country, for in 1562 he wrote to a Mr Thomas Windebank in Paris asking him to

(Above) The interior of the conservatory at Syon, built in 1827-30.
(Right) Paxton's 'Conservative Wall' at Chatsworth, designed for camellias.

procure 'a lemon tree, a pomegranate and a myrt', as he already had an orange. He also asked for instructions as to the 'ordering' of his trees and was told to stand them in a sheltered position in the summer, and bring them into the house between September and April. Sir Francis Carew of Beddington in Surrey bought his orange trees from France in the same year, again through Windebank's agency, but according to Evelyn had them 'planted in the open ground and sheltered in winter by a tabernackle of boards warmed by means of stoves'.

One of the first records of a 'house for orange trees' can be found in the accounts of the King's Works for 1611-12, describing the garden at Somerset House in the Strand, laid out by Salomon de Caus for Anne of Denmark. An engraving in de Caus's book *Les Raisons des forces mouvantes* (1615) shows a walk lined with orange and lemon trees in tubs with a vault beneath in which they passed the winter, and this may perhaps illustrate the projected arrangement at Somerset House. André Mollet's layout at Wimbledon, made for another Queen, Henrietta Maria, in the 1640s, gave the 'Orange Garden' much more prominence – with a loggia on the east side of the house leading into a sunken parterre where the trees would stand at the corners of the knots during the summer, sheltered by the surrounding walls, and where there was a large 'Orange-House', with south-facing windows, where they could be stored in the winter. The inventory taken by the Parliamentarians when they took over the house in 1649 lists sixty trees, all in tubs, forty-eight of them laden with fruit, as well as six pomegranates and a lemon – valued at the enormous sum of £420.

The expense and rarity of orange trees continued to make them a symbol of prestige throughout the seventeenth and eighteenth centuries. Although Charles II's marriage to Catherine of Braganza encouraged their importation through Portugal, Nell Gwynn's role as the orange-seller was a much more rarefied occupation than might be imagined. The Dutch East India Company was another source after William and Mary's accession, when orange trees also became a sign of loyalty to the Whig cause and the House of Orange. Samuel Pepys was so fascinated by Lord Brooke's oranges at Hackney, which he saw in June 1666, that he 'pulled off a little one by stealth and eat it' – and it was to prevent similar pilfering that Lord Burlington's orangery at Chiswick was 'separated from the Lawn by a Faussee, to secure the Orange-trees from being injured by Persons who are admitted to walk in the Garden'. Here, according to Defoe, 'they are seen as perfectly, and when the Orange-trees are in Flower, the Scent is diffused over the whole Lawn to the House'.

There is evidence that many of the open arcades of Elizabethan and Jacobean houses, as well as the loggias in their gardens, were glazed at a later date to act as orangeries, although many were unsuccessful due to their limited number of windows. This is certainly true of Burghley and Hatfield, and Sir William Temple, describing the two open loggias flanking the parterre at Moor Park (built in the 1630s), says that 'the Cloister facing the *South* is covered with Vines, and would have been proper for an Orange House, and the other for Myrtles, or other more common Greens . . . if this Piece of Gardening had been then in as much Vogue as it is now'. The usual form of the Georgian orangery, with arched windows, may have developed as much from this tradition, as from the need to provide the maximum amount of daylight.

Usually these buildings were simple in form, built of brick, with large-paned windows which could be unpegged and removed altogether in the summer months. The blank north wall often had flues built into it, and a series of small charcoal stoves kept hot air circulating through them in cold weather. Monsieur Beaumont's melon-ground at Levens had 'hot-beds' and heated frames working on the same principle as early as the 1690s, and the technique of fermenting tanbark also provided greater heat for forcing spring bulbs, acquired (at vast cost) from Holland. Much narrower versions of the normal orangery were also devised for growing grapes or figs, and their success can be judged from the Black Hamburg vine planted at Hampton Court in Queen Anne's reign, which still produces between five and six hundred bunches a year to be sold to the public.

Sometimes the central position occupied by an orangery in a garden, or the fact that it was joined on to the house itself, demanded a more architectural treatment. At Dyrham, the orangery was not only on axis with the long canal and cascade, but also directly adjoined the state apartment, allowing the smell of orange-blossom to waft through the rooms on the long west-front enfilade during the winter months. William Talman's façade was accordingly based on the grandest of prototypes, Hardouin-Mansart's Orangerie at Versailles, echoing the Grand Trianon with its channelled rustication and coupled columns. William Winde's great terraces at Powis Castle were modelled on another French palace, Saint-Germain-en-Laye, given to James II during his exile after 1688 – and here the central loggia (built for Henri IV) became a charming glazed orangery, whose parapet (surmounted by Van Nost's lead statues) acted as the balustrade for the terrace walk immediately above.

Timothy Nourse in *Campania Foelix* argues the case for greenhouses to be placed immediately under the terraced walk surrounding a sunk parterre (again as at Versailles), and lists as their 'Furniture', apart from the usual 'greens', '*Tuberosus's*, which will hold their Flowers in Winter, *Jessamins* of all sorts . . . as likewise *Mavyn*, *Syriacum*, which tho a little Shrub, or a sort of *Mastick Thyme*, is much to be valued for its rich Balsamick Smell: the Olive-Tree, the Pomegranate-Tree, the Oleander or Rose-Lawrel.' One of the largest and most ambitious of early greenhouses was that at Kensington Palace, designed by Nicholas Hawksmoor for Queen Anne in 1705. As grand as some of his City churches, it has an interior more like a sculpture gallery than a garden building, with rotundas at either end, giant Corinthian columns, and deep niches. Orange-trees and other 'greens' were evidently intended to be placed here with antique statuary, and the building used as a true 'winter garden' rather than simply a place of storage. Similar orangeries in Germany, including the Hanoverian Electors' at Herrenhausen, were used for concerts and theatrical performances in the summer months.

Most of the celebrated architects of the eighteenth century produced designs for greenhouses or orangeries at some stage in their career – from Wren and Vanbrugh to Wyatt and Holland. Both Vanbrugh's long Baroque greenhouse overlooking the east parterre at Blenheim, and Robert Adam's Neo-classical orangery-cum-sculpture-gallery at Bowood, were built to screen the stables from the house and garden, which partly explains their immense proportions. But that at Margam Abbey in South Wales, built in 1787-90 to the designs of Anthony Keck, is probably the largest of all – no less than 327 feet in length. Perhaps the sheer size of the building justified in its owner's eyes the old family tradition that the orange-trees were intended as a present from Philip II of Spain to Queen Elizabeth I, and were salvaged by his ancestor from a wreck off the Glamorgan coast.

Despite the fact that exotic blooms like orchids were introduced to England as early as the 1730s (in this case from the Bahamas), it was not until the very end of the century that glazed roofs were generally adopted, and it became easier to rear such hothouse plants. The breakthrough was achieved by the use of cast-iron for skylights in rooms like Nash's picture-gallery at Attingham. Inded, the same architect's conservatory at Barnsley Park, Gloucestershire – a free-standing Grecian temple, built in 1807, with cast-iron beams supporting a pitched roof of glass panes – was one of the first to employ the technology of the Industrial Revolution. Not far away at Sezincote, Sir Charles Cockerell, who had made a fortune in the service of the East India Company, commissioned his architect brother Samuel to remodel his house in the so-called Mughal style in 1805. The long curving greenhouse wing added to the south, leading to a pavilion which originally contained Sir Charles' bedroom, not only gave the house a picturesque asymmetry but also added to its Indian character with the delicate linear pattern of its repeated fanlights.

Humphry Repton, who was consulted about the house and garden at Sezincote, always recommended adding conservatories to houses in a suitable architectural style, rather than building them at a distance in the garden. One of the pairs of 'before' and 'after' plates in his *Observations* shows a dark, old-fashioned parlour contrasted with a Regency library-cum-drawing-room, opening out through double doors into a conservatory – while another shows a Gothic pavilion proposed in his 'Red Book' for Plas Newydd on the Isle of Anglesey, and described as 'a green-house, terminating a magnificent enfilade through a long line of principal apartments. The hint . . . taken from the chapter rooms to some of our cathedrals'. The ribs of the vault were to be of cast-iron with the interstices of glass, 'while the side window frames might be removed entirely in summer . . . when such a pavilion would tempt us to walk out by moonlight, to enjoy the murmur of the waves'.

Popular as winter gardens, glazed passages and domestic greenhouses remained throughout the Victorian period, advances in structural engineering, the invention of cheaper plate glass and the growing ambitions of botanical collectors resulted in the revival of the detached conservatory on a gigantic scale – particularly after the abolition of the tax on glass in 1845. One of the pioneers was Charles Fowler, architect of the Covent Garden covered market, whose domed conservatory at Syon built for the Duke of Northumberland in 1827-30 war large enough to contain full-sized forest trees. But the most famous was Joseph Paxton, the Duke of Devonshire's head-gardener, and creator of the 'Great Stove' or conservatory at Chatsworth erected between 1836 and 1840 – so huge that Queen Victoria and Prince Albert drove through it in a carriage and pair. It measured 292 feet by 130 feet, with a central dome rising to 71 feet and with 7035 square feet of glass, supported by 48 iron pillars. Unfortunately, its consumption of coal, brought in trucks through a tunnel under the pleasure garden, was so great that it was demolished in 1920, and only its low retaining walls survive – with a maze now planted within them. One of the great horticultural treasures of Chatsworth was the giant water-lily *Victoria amazonica*, which flowered for the first time in Britain in 1849, and the special house that Paxton built for it was modelled on the ribbed structure of its leaves. The 'Conservative Wall', a range of glasshouses climbing the steep hill to the stables, is all that now remains of his work, but it too looks forward to the engineering miracle of the Crystal Palace and the principles of the Modern Movement.

The conservatory at Flintham in Nottinghamshire, built by T.C. Hine in 1853 for Thomas Thoroton Hildyard, MP, was obviously inspired by the Crystal Palace. Rising the full height of the house, its conventional load-bearing walls support a barrel-vault of cast-iron and glass, but the end wall is a screen of stone tracery in imitation of cast-iron construction. The view of the great central fountain almost buried in exotic vegetation, seen through large plate-glass windows from the library, or from a Venetian-palazzo-style balcony at first-floor level, is one of the most bizarre and wonderful experiences that the Victorian country house has to offer.

By contrast the orangeries of Sir Edwin Lutyens and Sir Robert Lorimer returned for inspiration to the simple brick and stone forms of the seventeenth century, very often dispensing with glazed roofs altogether – and depending on greenhouse ranges concealed in the walled kitchen garden to produce the necessary citrus fruits and pot plants without having to worry about aesthetic considerations. The recent revival of more elaborate timber and cast-iron conservatories may never rival the achievements of the nineteenth century, due to the cost of upkeep, but they have brought back a welcome element of botanical experiment and architectural embellishment to the country-house gardens of the 1980s.

Robert Adam's garden house at Osterley, built about 1780.

*Italianate settings for Mediterranean plants: (above) Matthew Digby Wyatt's conservatory at Castle Ashby, 1861-65,
(below) the orangery at Blickling, built before 1793.*

*O*ne of the wings of the conservatory at Syon, designed by Charles Fowler,
architect of the covered market at Covent Garden, in 1827, and (right) the wooden orangery
at Saltram in Devon. It was built between 1773 and 1775 to house
orange trees brought back by Lord Boringdon from Genoa.

A fantasy for an East India Company nabob: the conservatory wing at Sezincote in Gloucestershire, designed by S.P. Cockerell for his brother, Sir Charles, about 1805. The delicate Mogul ornament may be due to the artist Thomas Daniell, who assisted the architect, and whose knowledge of Indian buildings was unrivalled.

XIII

TEMPLES AND EYECATCHERS

There can be few countries in the world where the garden building has taken on more various forms, or had more different associations, than in Britain. Classical temples or Gothick ruins, Chinese pagodas or Moorish deercotes, hermitages and dairies, obelisks and arches, they are united only by the idea of 'Nature improved by Art'. This wish to introduce human scale into the unformed landscape of the wild goes back to a primitive fear of the unknown, still very much alive in the classical world where temples were built in remote and isolated places to placate the gods.

Few of these garden buildings had a strictly utilitarian origin, except for dovecotes, which were a valuable source of food in the

(Above) An obelisk at Bramham Park in Yorkshire.
(Right) Athenian Stuart's Triumphal Arch at Shugborough, begun in 1761.

Middle Ages. Like the one at Athelhampton in Dorset with over a thousand nesting holes, these became a symbol of seigneurial power, since they could be built only by lords of the manor – a restriction that existed in France up to the Revolution. They also produced excellent manure, and for this reason were usually placed near kitchen gardens or melon grounds. The usual round shape with a conical roof also had a strictly practical basis: an entrance for the birds being provided either through an open lantern, or through small dormers in the roof, while eggs could be easily collected from the pigeonholes inside by means of a revolving yard-arm, or potence.

It is tempting to associate the circular form of so many later garden buildings with the dovecote, but there was an equal incentive to provide an architectural contrast both with the house and the rectangular plots of the formal parterre, and it is this that more often explains the strange geometrical shapes (as well as the eccentric styles) of the later 'folly'. The circular domed arbours seen in illuminated medieval manuscripts and in the backgrounds of Elizabethan portraits were usually made of timber, used as a framework for pleached lime, beech or hornbeam: a type that was to remain fashionable right up to the early eighteenth century. Occasionally their interiors were also netted so as to form aviaries, and there is evidence that the remarkable wrought-iron arbour at Melbourne, made by the blacksmith Robert Bakewell in 1710 and exactly imitating the trellis arbours of an earlier date, may have performed a similar function.

This combination of the natural and artificial – a kind of growing architecture – reached its most remarkable expression at Cobham Hall in Kent, where in 1629 John Parkinson saw a large lime tree whose branches were trained to form no less than three arbours, one above the other, in each of which 'might bee placed halfe an hundred men at the least'. A staircase joined the three storeys, and there were floorboards on the different levels, Parkinson concluding that it was 'the goodliest spectacle mine eyes ever beheld for one tree to carry'. Many more of these elaborate tree-houses once existed, but one of the few to survive is that at Pitchford Hall in Shropshire, with a room high up in the branches probably constructed in the seventeenth century, and given charming rococo plasterwork decoration by Thomas Farnolls Pritchard in the 1760s.

In the Elizabethan and Jacobean period, no large garden was complete without at least one banqueting house, built very like the turrets on the roof of the great house and used for similar purposes. At Hardwick, five of the towers which give it its unforgettable silhouette were used for banqueting – that is to say for different dessert courses laid out so that the company could move from one to another by turn – and in the garden little pavilions of much the same form, with strapwork cresting and flat roofs, performed the same function in the far corners of the walled garden. Those at Montacute were built in the angles of the forecourt, and again designed by the master-mason William Arnold in the same style as the house, because they formed part of a unified architectural composition. At Blickling, however, Robert Lyminge's design for a banqueting house, made about 1620, is in a remarkable mock-medieval style deliberately contrasting with the up-to-date Renaissance ornament of the house. With its castellations and loopholes, it can be compared with some of Inigo Jones' designs for stage sets – and indeed garden buildings were often conceived as backdrops for the masques and outdoor entertainments of the time.

The free flow of air, said to dispel evil 'humours', was obviously valued in an age prone to disease, and this was one of the reasons for siting banqueting houses on the tops of hills. Here, too, they could offer a view over the knots of the formal garden, or provide 'stands' to watch stag-hunting, hawking, coursing or horse-racing in progress. The hunting tower at Chatsworth, probably designed by Robert Smythson in the 1580s, has rooms on four floors, all provided with chimneypieces for the benefit of the spectators, and even in the flat countryside of East Anglia, the octagonal gazebo at Melford Hall is raised up on a mound at the edge of the garden, overlooking the approaches to the house.

In the late seventeenth century the great territorial magnates were generally so engrossed with the building of their houses that they had little time for elaborate garden pavilions, and in any case the dominance of the Baroque house over its surroundings – an expression of absolutist power – was not to be prejudiced by any of its satellites. William Talman's design for a 'Trianon' for William III at Hampton Court was to be built on a new site across the river, outside the orbit of the Palace, and at Blenheim the only 'eyecatcher' of any significance was the Column of Victory at the end of the Grand Avenue.

The third Earl of Carlisle, creator of Castle Howard, was one of the first to change this state of affairs, building Vanbrugh's Temple of the Winds and Hawksmoor's Mausoleum before work on the house itself had been completed. A third important feature of the landscape was the pyramid, and it is particularly interesting to find the anonymous author of a poem on Castle Howard (possibly the Earl's daughter, Lady Irwin) writing in 1733 that 'Buildings the proper points of view adorn,/Of *Grecian,*

Roman and *Egyptian* form' – a passage which makes it almost certain that the different styles of the three buildings were deliberately chosen to represent the great civilizations of the past – with Vanbrugh's palace representing the Whig supremacy, greatest of them all.

The stylistic associations of garden buildings were taken a step further by William Kent at Rousham, for here all the ornaments within the garden were in the classical vein, and all those outside – the mill, the 'eyecatcher' and even the remodelled house – were in a picturesque Gothic. This emphasis on the idea of a classical Elysium, far removed from native traditions, was strengthened by the many allusions to the antique, from Venus's Vale to Praeneste, the seven-arched portico built above the Cherwell, its named derived from the Roman Temple of Fortuna Virilis at Praeneste (now Palestrina), famous for its gigantic terraces.

At Stowe, the plethora of garden buildings erected by Lord Cobham, as if to illustrate his family motto 'Templa Quam Dilecta' (How Beautiful are thy Temples), had a more overtly political message. Thus, the Temple of Ancient Virtue in the little valley known as the Elysian Fields, laid out 'after Mr Kent's notion' about 1735, was a domed rotunda of the noblest simplicity, based on antique Roman sources, while the Temple of Modern Virtue was a mock-ruin: a comment on the supposed immorality of Walpole's government, then in power. At the same time the Temple of British Worthies, celebrating patriots from King Alfred and the Black Prince to Queen Elizabeth I and Shakespeare, Milton and Locke, proclaimed the nationalist, anti-Gallican sentiments of Lord Cobham's own Whig faction. The message was equally clear in Gibbs' polygonal Gothic Building, dating from the 1740s, and summoning up ancient Saxon traditions of liberty and democracy.

The associational value of the Gothic made it a suitable style for garden buildings even when the inspiration was purely pictorial or literary. Roger de Piles' *Cours de Peinture* of 1708, widely known in England even before it was translated in 1743, commented that 'Buildings in general are a great ornament in landskip, even when they are *Gothick*, or appear partly inhabited, and partly ruinous: they raise the imagination by the use they are thought to be designed for; as appears from antient towers, which seem to have been the habitations of fairies, and are now retreats for shepherds and owls'. Vanbrugh was one of the first to argue for the retention of a genuine ruin in his unsuccessful plea to the Duchess of Marlborough to preserve the remains of Old Woodstock Manor at Blenheim: not only 'raise'd by One of the Bravest and Most

Warlike of the English Kings', but also 'One of the Most Agreable Objects that the best of Landskip Painters can invent'.

In much the same way, Pope wished Lord Digby to incorporate the ruins of Sherborne Castle in his landscape garden: 'the open Courts from building to building might be thrown into Octagons of Grass or flowers, and even in the gaming Rooms, you have fine trees grown, that might be made a natural Tapistry to the walls, & arch you over-head where time has uncovered them to the Sky. Little paths of earth, or Sand, might be made, up the half-tumbled walls . . . & Seats placd here and there, to enjoy those views, which are more romantick than Imagination can form them.' Near the entrance, he suggested that an obelisk might be erected with an inscription telling of the castle's ancient origins and its destruction in the Civil War, a history doing 'no small honour' to the owner's family.

The ruins of Halesowen Abbey seen from Shenstone's garden at the Leasowes, and, above all, the view of Fountains Abbey from John Aislabie's garden at Studley Royal, show how successfully such buildings could be incorporated into the eighteenth-century landscape garden. But few owners were fortunate enough to have the real thing, and most had to be content with artificial ruins like Sanderson Miller's castle at Hagley, which Horace Walpole praised as having 'the true rust of the Barons' Wars' – or his less 'finished' Gothic Tower at Wimpole. Lord Hardwicke seems to have planned the latter as a deliberate contrast to 'Athenian' Stuart's Prospect Room, for engravings of the two were sent to his friends with a letter in which he wrote 'perhaps the views may strike you as no bad contrast between ancient and modern times'.

Because garden buildings were often set in isolated positions, not intended to be seen at the same time as any of their companions (a rule particularly stressed by William Gilpin), they were freed from architectural restraint to an even greater degree than lodges, and were often of a highly experimental nature. Stuart's Temple of Theseus at Hagley, designed in 1758, was the first Greek Revival monument in northern Europe, while the giant Pineapple at Dunmore in Stirlingshire, built by an unknown architect in 1761, has to be among the oddest buildings in the world. Another Neo-classical prototype which was greatly admired was the so-called 'Tower of the Winds' at Athens, published in Stuart and Revett's *Antiquities of Athens*, and versions of this were built both at Shugborough in Staffordshire and Mount Stewart in Northern Ireland. Others conceived in a spirit of archaeological enquiry included a whole class of 'primitive' buildings, from Adam's thatched hermitage at Kedleston with its rough tree-trunk columns, to Thomas Wright's root house at Badminton with an interior of bark and moss.

Some garden pavilions were specially designed as settings for *fêtes champêtres* like Nicholas Revett's Music Temple (early on described as a 'theatre') on an island in the lake at West Wycombe. Occasionally a dairy also provided a backdrop for the 'simple life' of shepherds and shepherdesses, reminiscent of Marie Antoinette's *hameau* at Versailles. The tenth Earl of Exeter, who married a farmer's daughter known as the 'Cottage Countess' – and the 70-year-old Sir Harry Fetherstonhaugh of Uppark who married an 18-year-old dairymaid – both had charming tiled milking parlours constructed for their wives. But the finest were Henry Holland's at Broadlands and Woburn Abbey, respectively in the Gothic and Chinese styles, and both still stocked with their original Wedgwood creamware.

As well as model farms, many houses had aviaries or menageries – ancestors of the public zoological gardens of the nineteenth century. At Horton in Northamptonshire the Earl of Halifax's contained storks, raccoons, two young tigers and a bear, as well as rare birds and fish, while Thomas Wright's pavilion (which also served as a belvedere overlooking the park) was appropriately decorated with the signs of the Zodiac in the plasterwork cove, and 'four great Urns representing the animals of the four parts of the World' in the niches below.

Towards the end of the eighteenth century, the refinement of the principles of 'Picturesque taste' led to simpler buildings, playing a less dominant role in a wilder landscape. The influence of the old masters is clear in Walpole's breathless description of Hagley: 'there is a hermitage, so exactly like those in Sadeler's prints [after Paul Brill], on the brow of a shady mountain, stealing peeps into the glorious world below! and there is such a pretty well under a wood, like the Samaritan woman's in a picture of Nicolò Poussin! . . . that I wore out my eyes with gazing, my feet with climbing, and my tongue and my vocabulary with commending!' Thomas Whateley in his *Observations on Modern Gardening* of 1770 takes this a stage further in a passage probably attacking the famous hermitage at Hawkstone, where a resident 'friar' was kept to read visitors' palms or appear rapt in meditation: 'a hermitage is the habitation of a recluse; it should be distinguished by its solitude and its simplicity; but if it is filled with crucifixes, hour-glasses, beads, and every other trinket which can be thought of, the attention is diverted from enjoying the retreat to examining the particulars . . . though each be natural, the collection is artificial'.

It was in an effort to avoid the artificial that Repton and his contemporaries often preferred cottages or farm-houses to more elaborate garden buildings. The 'Red Book' for Blaise Castle (of 1795-96) illustrates a cottage on the edge of a wood in the main view from the house, with the explanation: 'a temple or a pavilion in such a situation would receive the light and . . . would not appear to be inhabited, while this, by its form, will mark its intention, and the occasional smoke from the chimney will not only produce that cheerful and varying motion which painting cannot express, but it will frequently happen in a summer's evening that the smoke from this cottage will spread a thin veil along the glen, and produce that vapoury repose over the opposite wood which painters often attempt to describe . . .'.

The 'Old Cheshire' cottage at Biddulph Grange, Prince Albert's Swiss chalet at Osborne, and the whimsy bargeboarded fantasies of architects like George Devey, continued this tradition into the Victorian period. But with elaborate formal gardens round the house replacing the landscaped park, there was little future for the temple and the 'eyecatcher' in the old sense of the word. Lord Berners' folly at Faringdon, designed by the Duke of Wellington in 1935 – a 140-foot tower with an arcaded look-out room at the top – or Raymond Erith's circular folly at Gatley in Herefordshire, built in 1964, show that the tradition is not entirely dead. Even now, some financier with the right mixture of eccentricity and affluence, will be considering a pepperpot of reconstituted stone on some nearby hill and (one hopes) remembering Payne Knight's words:

> . . . harsh and cold the builder's work appears,
> Till soften'd down by long revolving years;
> Till time and weather have conjointly spread
> Their mould'ring hues and mosses o'er its head.

*T*he Mausoleum and (left) the Pyramid at Castle Howard,
both designed by Nicholas Hawksmoor in the 1720s. Their Grecian and
Egyptian forms may have been deliberately chosen to complement
Vanbrugh's Roman Temple of the Winds – thus representing the three
great civilisations of the past.

*F*rom *'fêtes champêtres' to funerals: (left) Henry Flitcroft's Pantheon at Stourhead, seen across the lake; (above) Sir John Vanbrugh's domed rotunda at Duncombe Park in Yorkshire; and (below) Joseph Bonomi's mausoleum at Blickling in Norfolk, burial place of the earls of Buckinghamshire.*

*V*isions of Elysium: (above) the temple and obelisk in Lord Burlington's orange tree garden at Chiswick, (below) William Kent's Temple of British Worthies at Stowe, and (right) his seven-arched portico at Rousham, called Praeneste after the Roman temple at Palestrina. Dating from the 1720s and 1730s, such buildings were in the vanguard of the Palladian movement.

*D*ovecotes may have inspired the circular garden buildings of later generations:
(above) the stone-tiled pigeon house at Nymans, and the interior of a seventeenth-century
example at Rousham, showing the yard-arm used to reach the nesting boxes.
(Left) The dome of Robert Bakewell's wrought-iron arbour at Melbourne in Derbyshire.

*T*he 'true rust of the Barons' Wars': (left) Sanderson Miller's ruined castle at Wimpole;
(above) Batty Langley's hexagon temple at Bramham; and (below) the view from Charles Hamilton's gothick
temple at Painshill in Surrey. The pleasing melancholy of mock-ruins, and the associational
value of the Gothic, as an expression of ancient liberties and national pride, made it a popular style for
garden buildings in the mid-eighteenth century.

XIV

PARKS AND PLANTATIONS

It used to be thought that the park or 'pleasance' developed from the enclosure of hunting grounds in the Middle Ages, and that it was never deliberately planted with trees until after the Renaissance. However, recent research has shown that the modern idea of the landscaped park arrived in England very much earlier, and was almost certainly brought from the Middle East by the Norman crusaders. Thus Geoffrey de Montbray, Bishop of Coutances, who had himself been as far as southern Italy, bought a large estate in Normandy from William the Conqueror and, in the words of a contemporary, 'surrounded the park with a double ditch and a palisade. Within he sowed acorns and took pains to grow oaks and beeches and other forest trees, filling the park with deer from England'.

(Left) The park at Chatsworth, seen from the Elizabethan hunting tower.
(Above) Cedars of Lebanon at Osterley in Middlesex.

By 1110, Henry I had enclosed Woodstock Park with a stone wall, and as well as visiting the manor frequently for the hunting, kept a menagerie of wild animals there, including a porcupine. Planting was almost certainly carried out with aesthetic as well as sporting considerations in mind, although the idea of woods with straight rides cut through them (often meeting at *rond-points*) was the rule for stag or wild boar hunts until the early eighteenth century. Pheasants were introduced to England by at least 1355 when a boy was paid twopence by Elizabeth de Burgh for carrying three of them from her castle at Clare in Suffolk to her park nearby at Bardfield. But these were kept for interest rather than for sport, and pheasant-shooting was not seriously considered for another 400 years.

Specimen trees, many of them again brought from the Middle East and the Mediterranean countries, were being planted in parks, outside the garden proper, by at least the sixteenth century. Henry Hawkins in his *Parthenia Sacra* of 1633 gives them an emblematic significance, just as much as flowers – including '*the Cedar of high* Contemplation, *the* Cypres *of odiferous* fame *and* Sanctitie *of life, the* Laurel *of* Constancie, *the* Almond *of* Fruitfulnes' and the 'Plane-tree *of* Fayth'. Silviculture too was beginning to be recognized as a profitable business with the ever-increasing demands of the navy and the building industry – particularly in the period of the Dutch Wars, and during the reconstruction of London after the Great Fire.

John Evelyn's *Sylva, or a Discourse of Forest Trees*, published in 1664 with many practical tips on the subject, went into four editions in his lifetime, and it would be hard to find a country-house library today without a copy. Indeed it is no exaggeration to say that the plantations made by the great territorial magnates (often on the most unpromising terrain) changed the face of the British countryside in the late seventeenth and early eighteenth centuries. Charles Cotton in his poem *The Wonders of the Peake* (1681), seeing the park at Chatsworth 'environ'd round with *Natures* Shames, and Ills,/Black Heaths, wild Rocks, bleak Craggs, and naked Hills', concludes 'that this is *Paradice*, which seated stands/In midst of *Desarts*, and of barren *Sands*'. Siberechts' painting of the house about 1710 shows what he means, for the bare moorland above it looks almost like a lunar landscape, and – despite much further planting – there is the same extraordinary contrast coming over the hills from Chesterfield today.

In similar fashion, Daniel Defoe described the 'great Improvement' at Painshill in the early eighteenth century 'by enclosing a large Tract of Land designed for a Park, which was most of it so poor as not to produce anything but *Heath* and *Broom*; but by burning of the *Heath*, and spreading of the Ashes on the Ground, a Crop of *Turneps* was obtained; and by feeding Sheep on the *Turneps*, their Dung became a good Manure to the Land, so that a good Sward of Grass is now upon the Land, where it was judged by most People impossible to get any Herbage'. Agricultural improvements and land reclamation by later landlords, such as Coke of Norfolk, were to make virtually any kind of soil seem possible for the creation of parks and plantations.

On the whole, straight lines were still preferred outside as well as inside the formal garden at the turn of the seventeenth century, which helps explain why bird's-eye view paintings (stressing the geometrical effects of woods and ridings) were still much more popular than compositions made on the ground. Kent's treatment of trees was revolutionary in this context, just as his use of water had been. At Rousham, the waving edges of the woodland were sometimes underplanted with shrubs to achieve a pictorial effect, sometimes treated as open groves with the bare trunks giving the effect of a stage perspective. At other times, 'where the united plumage of an ancient wood extended wide its undulating canopy, and stood venerable in its darkness', Walpole records that 'Kent thinned the foremost ranks, and left but so many detached and scattered trees, as softened the approach of gloom and blended a chequered light with the thus lengthened shadows of the remaining columns'.

Though praising his painterly eye, Walpole also criticized Kent's clumps as too puny: describing them on one occasion as making a lawn 'look like the ten of spades', and on another complaining that 'he aimed at an immediate effect, and planted not for futurity . . . how common to see three or four beeches, then as many larches, a third knot of cypresses, and a revolution of all three!' On the other hand, Joseph Spence wrote that 'Mr Kent always used to stake out his grovettes before they planted, and view the stakes every way, to see that no three of them stand in a line'. Capability Brown, as a practical plantsman, was to be more successful in the creation of spinneys, coppices and woods on a large scale, and seeing his trees grown to full maturity – as in the park at Petworth, immortalized by Turner – one can almost forgive him for the destruction of so many earlier formal layouts. At Stowe, where Brown served his apprenticeship, the planting reflects many of his later 'tricks of the trade', notably the way in which the trees planted on the flanking ridges of the Grecian Valley seem to deepen its contours – as Thomas Jefferson noticed on his visit in 1786.

Brown is often credited with the invention of the circuit walk or drive, taking the visitor on a serpentine route round the edge of the park, usually by way of the highest points so as to produce a series of varied viewpoints *en route*. He certainly made wide use of this feature, though he was by no means the first to do so. For instance Stephen Switzer had already laid down the guidelines in the 'Prooemial Essay' to his *Ichnographia Rustica* of 1742: 'I have one more thing to add, as to Design, which has been generally omitted by all that have wrote, and by many that have practised Rural and Extensive Gardening; and that is the Ambit, Circuit, or Tour . . . such as in all large Designs can be only done on Horseback, or in a Chaise or Coach . . . This *Anfilade* or Circuit ought to be six or seven Yards wide at least, and should be carried over the tops of the highest Hills that lie within the Compass of any Nobleman's or Gentleman's Design . . . and from these Eminencies (whereon, if anywhere, Building or Clumps of Trees ought to be placed) it is that you are to view the whole Design'.

Robert Adam's sketch for the pleasure ground at Kedleston shows just such a circuit walk, eventually extended to a length of over three miles, enclosing paddocks for 'Scotch cattle' and 'Indian deer'. According to William Gilpin, 'the most natural inhabitants of parks are fallow deer; and very beautiful they are: but flocks of sheep, and herds of cattle are more useful; and in my opinion more beautiful. Sheep particularly are very ornamental in a park. Their colour is just that dingy hue, which contrasts with the verdure of the ground; and the flakiness of their wool is rich, and picturesque'. At Strawberry Hill, Horace Walpole delighted in his 'enamelled meadows . . . speckled with cows, horses and sheep', reminding one of his friends how important it was to have three or four cows (as in the paintings of Cuyp and Potter), since 'two cows can't group'. The way in which the cattle trimmed the lower branches of the trees to an even height – allowing views through to sun-dappled pasture or the glinting surface of a lake – was another feature of the eighteenth-century park, still very much in evidence.

One of the most important developments during the Georgian period was the introduction of new species from every quarter of the globe. As regards trees, Walpole paid special tribute to the third Duke of Argyll, patron of many botanical expeditions, for 'the mixture of various greens, the contrast of forms between our forest-trees and the northern and West-Indian firs and pines', giving 'the richness of colouring so peculiar to our modern landscape'. Thus it was possible to effect changes of mood by planting, as Spence suggested in 1751 – 'to observe the different friendships and enmities of different colours, and to place the most friendly ones next each other'; or, 'in the mixing of lights and shades, to let the former have the prevalence, or, in other words, to give the whole a joyous air rather than a melancholy one'.

In the nineteenth century, the great arboretums like Westonbirt, founded in 1829, or Scone in 1852, encouraged the cultivation of rare specimens for their own sake, rather than as part of an overall planting scheme. Hanging woods like those at Goodwood continued to be planted for pheasant-shooting, offering high birds to the guns placed in the valley below, but for the most part forestry became a more commercial affair, with outlying tracts of conifers unhappily replacing hardwoods early in this century. At the same time the essential conservatism of the English landowner has ensured that trees are rarely cut down until they need to be, and even then that replanting and regeneration are carried out in the old manner.

Just as the interior of the country house represents layer on layer of taste, with every generation leaving its mark, so the views from its windows, over ancient oaks and 'Capability' clumps, to blue woods on the far horizon, speak of continuity in a changing world. As the heroine of Jane Austen's *Emma* observed, looking out over the old park at Donwell with 'its abundance of timber in rows and avenues, which neither fashion nor extravagance had rooted up . . . it was a sweet view – sweet to the eye and the mind. English verdure, English culture, English comfort, seen under a sun bright, without being oppressive.'

A massive sycamore tree in the park at Drumlanrig Castle, Dumfriesshire, probably planted in the late seventeenth century, and (above) a detail of its trunk.

*T*he variety of hard and soft woods found in Britain give its parks, in Walpole's
words, 'the richness of colouring so peculiar to our modern landscape':
(left) beeches at Bowood in Wiltshire; (above) silver birches at Thorp Perrow
in Yorkshire, and an ancient oak at Cholmondeley Castle, Cheshire.

Animals as ornaments: (left) sheep in the park at Blenheim, (above) deer at Charlecote in Warwickshire, where Shakespeare is said to have been caught poaching; (below) pigs on the Home Farm at Shugborough, and a Highland bull at Tyninghame. The trimming of the lower branches by cattle was an important feature of the eighteenth-century landscape park.

*M*ist hangs in the valley below
Castle Drogo, Devon, Sir Edwin
Lutyens' twentieth-century
masterpiece.

INDEX

Right: British gardens featured in this book open to the public

Main map (England, Wales, Scotland):

Kinross

Tyninghame

GLASGOW   EDINBURGH

SCOTLAND   BERWICK

Floors Castle

Drumlanrig Castle

Cragside

NEWCASTLE

CARLISLE

ENGLAND

Mount Stewart

ISLE OF MAN

Holker Hall   Levens Hall

Thorp Perrow   SCARBOROUGH

Studley Royal   Duncombe Park

Castle Howard

YORK

Bramham Park

Harewood House   Temple Newsam House   HULL

LEEDS   Nostell Priory

MANCHESTER

ANGLESEY   SHEFFIELD

Tatton Park

LIVERPOOL

Biddulph Grange   Chatsworth

Plas Newydd   Bodnant   Hardwick Hall

Penrhyn Castle   Cholmondeley Castle   Haddon Hall   Newstead Abbey

Erddig Park   Alton Towers   Flintham Hall

Chirk Castle   Kedleston Hall   Wollaton Hall

Sudbury Hall   DERBY   Holkham Hall

Shugborough   Belvoir Castle   Grimsthorpe Castle   Blickling Hall

Powis Castle   Attingham Park   Calke Abbey   NORWICH

Melbourne Hall   Burghley House

LEICESTER   PETERBOROUGH

WALES   Hagley   BIRMINGHAM

Packwood House   Boughton House

Charlecote   Holdenby House   Lamport Hall

Farnborough Hall   Canons Ashby   Castle Ashby   Anglesey Abbey

Hidcote Manor   Stowe   CAMBRIDGE   IPSWICH

Sezincote   Rousham   Woburn Abbey   Wimpole Hall

GLOUCESTER   Blenheim Palace   Waddesdon Manor   Wrest Park   Melford Hall

Westbury Court   Ashridge Park

Cirencester Park   OXFORD   Hatfield House

SWANSEA   Barnsley Park   Nuneham Courtenay   Gorhambury

Margam Abbbey   Badminton House   Bowood   Cliveden   LONDON

CARDIFF   Blaise Castle   West Wycombe Park   Cobham Hall

BRISTOL   Dyrham Park   Corsham Court   Painshill

BATH   Ashdown House

Buscot Park   Hever Castle   Penshurst Place   DOVER

Hestercombe   Stourhead   Heale House   Nymans   Scotney Castle   Sissinghurst Castle

Tintinhull Manor   Wilton   Uppark   Leonardslee   Great Dixter

Knightshayes   Montacute   SOUTH-AMPTON   Broadlands   Sheffield Park

Cranborne Manor   Petworth House   Parham

Exbury   PORTSMOUTH   Goodwood   BRIGHTON

Castle Drogo   EXETER   Osborne

ISLE OF WIGHT

PLYMOUTH   Saltram House

PENZANCE

Scotland inset (top right):

Dunrobin Castle

Pitmedden

INVERNESS   Craigievar   ABERDEEN

SCOTLAND   Crathes Castle

Blair Castle   Edzell Castle

Drummond Castle   PERTH

London inset (bottom right):

LONDON

Moor Park

Chiswick House   Kenwood

Richmond Palace

Kew Gardens

Osterley Park   Richmond Park, White Lodge

Syon Park   Ham House

Hampton Court Palace

Claremont

223